Tell *Her* Story

Tell *Her* Story

A History of Women in Missions

Darline Royer with Elizabeth Z. Turner

Word Aflame Press®
36 Research Park Court
Weldon Spring, MO 63304
pentecostalpublishing.com

Excerpts from *Sent! Volume 3: A History of UPCI Global Missions, Africa* have been adapted and included in this manuscript with the permission of the publisher.

An excerpt from William Turner's *The Church on Godless Lane: Missionary Stories from Russia and the Former Soviet Union* has been adapted and included in this book with the permission of the author.

An excerpt from William D. Turner's *India to the World: The Missionary Pilgrimage of Harry E. Scism* has been adapted and included in this book with the permission of the author.

Cover design by Mandy DeHart
Printed in the United States of America

Library of Congress Cataloging-in-Publication Data

Names: Royer, Darline Kantola, 1936- author. | Turner, Elizabeth Z., author.
Title: Tell her story : a history of women in missions / by Darline Royer and Elizabeth Z. Turner.
Description: Weldon Spring, Missouri : Word Aflame Press, [2024] | "Excerpts from Sent Vol. 3: A History of Global Missions, Africa have been adapted and included in this manuscript by permission of the publisher." | Includes bibliographical references. | Summary: "A history of single women missionaries in the United Pentecostal Church International"-- Provided by publisher.
Identifiers: LCCN 2024024797 (print) | LCCN 2024024798 (ebook) | ISBN 9780757766046 (paperback) | ISBN 9780757766053 (epub)
Subjects: LCSH: Missionary stories. | United Pentecostal Church International--Missions. | Women missionaries.
Classification: LCC BV2087 .R69 2024 (print) | LCC BV2087 (ebook) | DDC 266/.99409252--dc23/eng/20240628
LC record available at https://lccn.loc.gov/2024024797
LC ebook record available at https://lccn.loc.gov/2024024798

Dedication

This book is dedicated to Else Lund in recognition of her forty-two years of faithful missionary ministry and as a tribute to all the single women who have served as missionaries of the United Pentecostal Church International. Else exemplifies the fifty-plus single missionary ladies who have labored under the UPCI Global Missions umbrella since 1945, plus over one hundred Apostolic missionary women going back to the early 1900s. It is inspiring to also note that a host of young women have served in short-term missions since the inauguration of the Associate in Missions (AIM) program over forty years ago. Many of those women in short-term missions went on to full-time missionary appointments. Some remained single, and others later married and continued in missionary service.

Contents

PART V EUROPE and MIDDLE EAST

Preface

By Darline Royer

When William Turner, Dorsey Burk, and Darline Royer met as a committee authorized by former Global Missions Director Bruce Howell to compile a history of UPCI Global Missions, their discussions birthed the question: "What roles have single women played in the story of Apostolic global missions?" The challenge was to provide an authentic answer. When the committee gave me the task of compiling the story of single women in UPCI missions, I began looking for information about missionaries of bygone years and requesting information from retired and current missionaries. A few months later the committee decided that I should instead begin compiling the history of missionaries to Africa.

After completing the manuscript about Africa, I returned to the unfinished manuscript about women in missions. At that juncture, I felt impressed to invite Elizabeth Turner, a former missionary, published writer, and English teacher, to help with the writing of the book. Thus, Elizabeth and I became writing partners. At times I offer my own personal observations; all such instances in the book are from my experience and perspective.

This book serves as a stand-alone volume of the history of UPCI Global Missions. While the three volumes in the *SENT!* series include information about single women who were appointed and supported by the UPCI, this book expands on their contributions to global missions as an incentive for women to answer God's call today. The previous volumes are as follows:

SENT! Volume 1, A History of UPCI Global Missions, Asia, Europe/Middle East, Central America/Caribbean, by William D. Turner (2020).

SENT! Volume 2, A History of UPCI Global Missions, South America and the Pacific, by Dorsey Burk (2021).

SENT! Volume 3, A History of UPCI Global Missions, Africa, by Darline Royer (2022).

The primary published resources that provided information about missionaries of past years are as follows (see bibliography for a more complete list):

Insight, Foreign Missions Directory (many editions)—Compiled and edited by Dorsey Burk

The Foreign Missions Story by Foreign Missions Division (issues 1971–1976)

The Evolving World of Foreign Missions—by Daniel L. Scott Sr.

Apostolic Pioneers in Missions—by Dorsey L. Burk

Profiles of Pentecostal Missionaries—compiled by Mary Wallace

Sarah and Her Missionary Daughters—by Bonnie Markham

I Surrender All—by Pauline Gruse with Charles Clanton

Thanks to the diligent work of these writers, the records verify that single women have played a significant role in missions from the early decades of the twentieth-century Apostolic awakening. As these women experienced New Testament salvation (and in some cases even before), they answered God's call to share His Word in distant lands.

Introduction

Women in UPCI Global Missions

Before the United Pentecostal Church was established, single women played a significant role in planting the Apostolic message in China, India, Ecuador, and Liberia. Some of these women learned about and received the Holy Ghost and baptism in Jesus' name after they arrived on foreign soil. Pentecostal organizations sent some of these women; others became "faith missionaries," trusting God for their finances.

These early missionaries received their support from three leading Pentecostal organizations: (1) Pentecostal Assemblies of the World (PAW); (2) Pentecostal Church Incorporated (PCI); and (3) Pentecostal Assemblies of Jesus Christ (PAJC). The PCI and PAJC merged in 1945 to form the United Pentecostal Church (UPC). In 1972 the word *International* was added, and the organization is now commonly referred to as the UPCI.

A search of the PAW records by Daniel Scott provided valuable insights. He stated, "The PAW was the first organization that facilitated the Oneness missionary program."[1] The names of single women who adhered to Apostolic doctrine appear in the PAW missionary listings and on multiple disbursement lists of the early 1900s.

A review of the PAW list of missionaries sent to China by 1920 reveals an impressive number of single women. The names of thirteen women assigned to North and South China by or before 1920 appear in the PAW's 1920 publication, *Voice in the Wilderness.*

A review of the PCI and PAJC records also shows significant involvement of single women in pioneer missionary work. A report on the 1933 PCI Conference listed twenty-four missionary appointments (counting each couple as one).[2] Nine of these appointments were single ladies: May Iry, Elizabeth Stieglitz, Elsie G. King, Dorothy McCarty, Louise Dickson, Lotti Hatcher, Emma Reynolds, Helen Beldon, and Louise Olsen. The merger of the PCI and the PAJC resulted in some of these women continuing their missionary work as UPC-appointed missionaries. *Profiles of Pentecostal Missionaries* provides information about some of these early Apostolic missionaries.[3]

In his September 1947 report to the UPC General Board, Foreign Missions Secretary Wynn Stairs stated that the Foreign Missions Board was supporting forty missionaries in nine countries. The missionary roster included eleven single women, representing 27 percent of the missionary constituency. These eleven women were appointed to six countries in three continents: Africa, Asia, and South America.

China—Elizabeth Stieglitz, Kathryn Hendricks, and Mae Iry
Liberia—Georgia Regenhardt and Gladys Robinson
India—Dorothy "Mother" McCarty and Telie Dover
Java—Edith Berthoux
Colombia—Grace Ball
Palestine—Louise Dickson and "Sister" Hogg[4]

Though personal accounts of some of these women were not found, the list verifies that single women figured prominently in early UPC missionary work.

As I read and compiled the stories of the women who have served in missions, I was amazed by how God chose, called, and equipped women of various ages and backgrounds.

Some women answered God's call as young adults and put aside the prospect of marriage.

Others felt called at a young age and drifted from God's plan. God reached for them again after marriage, hardships, and divorce, and sent them into missions. Some went to the field as single ladies, but in God's plan and time, they married and returned to the field with a husband. Others went to the field married, but after their spouse passed away, they returned to the field single to carry on their mission work.

Some early missionary ladies responded to God's call before they heard about the Pentecostal experience. While on the field, they heard about and received the Holy Ghost and were baptized in Jesus' name. Many early missionary ladies in Liberia who worked as mission-station teachers often faced difficulties and inconveniences. Along with teaching, they provided pastoral leadership and evangelized in the villages.

Blending their global stories into one book with logical chapter divisions has proved challenging. In one sense, each missionary lady represents the dedication of all these precious God-called women. It has been my delight to know many of these women personally, even some of the early missionaries. As a ten-year-old child, I had the honor of meeting Georgia Regenhardt. At the time, she was attending Pentecostal Bible Institute before her appointment to Liberia in 1946. I met Ena Hylton (a missionary to Liberia) when she attended Conquerors Bible College, where I taught. My years as a missionary and recent involvement with the Global Association of Theological Studies (GATS) have allowed me to know many of these missionary ladies.

The missionary experiences of these extraordinary ladies could fill many volumes. Hopefully, the glimpses of their lives contained in this book will glorify the God who called them and influence today's women to heed God's call. The style and content of these missionary stories vary considerably. Some stories are brief due to the sparse information available. Longer stories were compiled from data found in UPCI publications or missionary books. The more detailed reports, which provide insights about a missionary's background, calling, appointment, and experiences on the field, resulted from discussions and correspondence with veteran and current missionaries. The writers express their gratefulness to those who wrote their own stories. As the reader will note, some stories are shared in first person, and other stories have been changed to third person by the writers/compilers, Darline and Elizabeth.

1

Else Lund's Story

"Queen of the United Pentecostal Church of Ghana" Liberia, Ghana, and Other Countries

Else Lund answered the call to Liberia in 1962 and continued her missionary work for forty-two years. In September 2014, Else Lund was honored by the UPCI Order of the Faith. Her story, as shared at the Order of the Faith banquet, exemplifies the calling and dedication of single lady missionaries who have served under appointment with the UPCI. Her story portrays those who have followed the "planters" to assist in developing Apostolic believers. From 1962 until 2004, Else faithfully continued her global ministry as a teacher and preacher of God's Word. Her years of service, spanning more than four decades, place her among the longest-serving missionaries of the UPCI.

Else applied for an appointment to Africa as a teacher. She replaced Pauline Gruse, who was retiring after twenty years as a teacher at the Fassama Mission school. Daniel Scott commented about her photo in the May 1963 *Pentecostal Herald*: "Else Lund appears young and vibrant as she departs for the field to begin her missionary service in Liberia."[1] Through the years, Else transitioned to being a Bible school teacher and was active in many aspects of evangelism and church growth.

From 1998 until her retirement in 2004, Else's appointment included International Teaching Ministry.

During her forty-two years as a missionary, she served in six West African countries (Liberia, Ghana, Nigeria, Senegal, Ivory Coast, and Togo) and three East African countries (Kenya, Uganda, and Tanzania). Additionally, she ministered in Scotland and Denmark.

While her story and the longevity of her missionary service are worthy of their own book, the summary of her life (with minor adaptations), as shared at the 2014 UPCI Order of the Faith banquet, gives a glimpse of her remarkable life and missionary labor.

Else Lund's father was born in Denmark and her mother in Norway, but they met and married in Canada. Else, their first child, was born a year later, on September 16, 1932, in Dyment, Ontario, Canada. Two other children, a son named Ralph and a daughter named Ingeborg, were born within the next few years.

At age five, Else began her education in a one-room country school. She and another girl were the only students in the first grade. When the children finished their work, the teacher often allowed them to look at *The Books of Knowledge*, one of which contained pictures of Africa. Else loved that book so much that she returned to it repeatedly. She later understood why it drew her. When she was fifteen, she told her dad she wanted to be a missionary. He immediately replied, "No, you are not going to live the life that a missionary would have to live." Brokenhearted with her father's answer, she wept and could not understand why she felt so bad.

Else graduated from high school in Dryden, Ontario, in 1950. She then began teaching in a two-room school in Dinorwic, Ontario. During summer vacation, she attended Ontario College of Teachers in Toronto. After completing that course, she continued taking courses at Ryerson

Institute of Technology during her summer vacations. Her goal was to obtain a degree in teaching and become a high school teacher. However, her life took a sudden turn when she contracted polio during the epidemic of 1953. Ten days later, Ralph and Ingeborg also became ill. Because of the epidemic, there was no room in the area hospitals, so Else was sent by train to a hospital in Sudbury.

Paralyzed from the neck down, Else was unable to do anything for herself. She spent nine months in the hospital, praying the only way she knew how to pray—by reciting the Lord's Prayer. When she finally was able to walk again and care for herself after a fashion, hospital personnel told her they could do nothing more for her and sent her home. She remained under quarantine, as did all those suffering from polio. One day, a pastor opened the door of her room and said, "This has happened for a purpose." Else never forgot his words. How true they were! It was polio that brought the Lund family to the Lord.

Else returned to teaching in 1954. At that time, she was invited to a meeting in the Edward Kelbert home. This was the beginning of the United Pentecostal Church in Dryden. In 1955, she and Ingeborg repented at the Kenora UPC, pastored by William Cooling. Later, Pastor Cooling baptized her in the name of Jesus Christ at Bethel Tabernacle in Winnipeg. Realizing the Lord was leading her in another direction, Else was no longer intent on continuing to teach or pursue a degree. An opportunity opened to minister in the Dinorwic Indian Reserve, now known as Wabigoon Lake First Nations. Before long, she realized God was calling her to Africa, a place she had loved since she was in the first grade. Her calling was strong; she lived only to go to Africa. She attended Apostolic Bible Institute in St. Paul, Minnesota, and graduated in 1962. In October

1962, she received a missionary appointment to Fassama, Liberia, West Africa.

In March 1963, Else sailed from Brooklyn, New York, on the *African Glen*, a commercial ship. The only other passenger on the three-week journey was an older missionary lady returning to Liberia. She advised Else on missionary work, which later proved most helpful. Else believes the Lord arranged their meeting.

Else faced many challenges in Liberia, but the Lord took her victoriously through them all. Twice, she faced danger when flying on the Sheaves for Christ Piper Cub. Once they were lost in fog over the jungle. Another time the brake cable unraveled as they landed, causing the plane to crash. Shortly after a coup, she almost lost her new Sheaves for Christ car. A tall, heavily armed soldier was inspecting Else's identification card when a short, slender man clothed in travel attire stepped up. The soldier clicked his heels and stood frozen at attention. The shorter man took Else's ID card out of the soldier's hand, handed it to Else, and said, "This is all she requires." His words were so quiet and gentle that she relaxed. After he repeated the exact words at least three times, Else realized she was free to go. They later searched for the gentleman, trying to learn who he was. Nobody knew. Else felt sure God had sent an angel to deliver her that day.

In February 1971, Else transferred to Accra, Ghana, to teach in the Bible school that had been opened by Missionary R. K. Rodenbush. During her service in Ghana, she also ministered in Liberia, Nigeria, Senegal, and Ivory Coast. In 1989, Else returned to Liberia to work in the Bible school while the Jim Hall family was on deputation. In May 1990, she had to evacuate due to the civil war. She packed two suitcases and hastily boarded the last flight of

Ghana Airways. The airline left one suitcase behind, so the only bag she had was the one with her books and teaching notes. Back in Ghana, she plunged into refugee work and helped build a church in the refugee camp. One of her Bible school students from Liberia, a refugee himself, pastored the work.

In 1998, Else was appointed to International Teaching Ministries and taught in Kenya, Uganda, Tanzania, Togo, and Scotland. She also spent six months helping to start a church in Copenhagen, Denmark. In November 2004, after forty-two years of service, she felt it was the Lord's will to retire from Global Missions. She now resides in her hometown of Dryden, Ontario, Canada, where she continues to share the gospel with those she meets.

In summing up her missionary years, Else stated, "If I had the opportunity, I would do the same thing again."

PART I
ASIA

2

China, Before and After 1945

Elizabeth Stieglitz, Mae Iry, Kathryn Hendricks, Virginia Weddle, Alice Kugler (Sheets)

With the dawn of the twentieth century, China emerged as a major country where missionaries felt called to share the gospel of Jesus Christ despite difficulties and dangers. Among those feeling the urgency to plant truth in China were many single women. Their stories display courage and commitment while sharing the gospel of Jesus Christ amid hardships. We now understand why so many people answered God's call to China in the first half of the twentieth century, because the rise of communism closed China's door to Christian missions later in the century.

Some names of single lady missionaries to China listed by early Oneness organizations are as follows: Olive E. Maw to South China (1916 PAW roster); Alma Hunt and Elizabeth Stieglitz to North China; Georgia Cound, Alice Kugler, and Carry Anderson to South China (1920 PAW Missionaries on the field, *Voice in the Wilderness*); Mae Iry to North China (1921 PAW list and 1947 UPC list); Kathryn E. Hendricks to North China (1946 UPC report),[1] and Elsie G. King (1933 PCI list). A search of available records did not provide information about some of these early missionaries; however, early missionary work in China by single women is amply documented by a few brief biographies. Before the 1945 merger of the PCI and PAJC to form the UPC, the following women missionaries to China served under other Oneness groups. They served as appointed missionaries with the United Pentecostal Church after the 1945 merger.

Elizabeth Stieglitz (early 1900s)

Profiles of Pentecostal Missionaries includes the impressive story of Elizabeth Stieglitz, a young lady who felt called to China in her teen years.[2] Her spiritual quest began in 1902 at age thirteen when God healed her of a large goiter. Deeply touched, she told God she would dedicate the rest of her life to Him if He also would heal her mother of heart disease, tuberculosis, and other disorders. Her mother agreed to attend a tent meeting held by Maria Woodworth-Etter. She attended and received complete healing.

In 1908, Elizabeth heard about meetings by William Durham in Chicago where people had received the Holy Ghost with the evidence of speaking in other tongues. Elizabeth attended the meeting and prayed herself into exhaustion, seeking to be filled with the Spirit. After a week, someone counseled her to get some rest. After resting, she awakened with waves of God's Spirit sweeping over her. She spoke in tongues for hours.[3]

As a twenty-year-old Spirit-filled believer feeling a call to China, Elizabeth accompanied a missionary couple named Ramsey to China in 1910. They launched their missionary labor by faith, trusting God for their needs. The three arrived in Shanghai and then traveled inland via a two-wheeled cart pulled by mules. They reached the site of a Swedish Holiness Mission, where they stayed until they found their own place. Sporadic revolutions interrupted their work; however, they remained in China, enduring hardships. After prolonged seasons of fervent prayer, God began to pour out His Spirit. According to Elizabeth's story, "The prayer meetings evolved into three glorious services a day, and at least four people received the Holy Ghost daily over the next four years with few exceptions."[4]

In 1914, Elizabeth read about baptism in Jesus' name in Frank Ewart's *Meat in Due Season* publication, which she received in the mail. She initially resisted the message of Jesus Name baptism until God spoke to her: "You are kicking against My name." Ultimately, the missionaries and all the church people accepted baptism in Jesus' name.[5]

In 1917, before Elizabeth could take her first furlough, she nearly died from typhus. The Ramseys sent word to her parents that they did not think she could possibly live. However, she survived and returned to the States for furlough, though desperately weak. Younger missionaries manned the mission while Elizabeth and the aging Ramseys took their furloughs. When Elizabeth returned to China, she faced cruel disappointment. Misdeeds by the ones left in charge resulted in non-Pentecostals taking over the mission and the cessation of the Holy Ghost revival. However, she and two believers moved on to an untouched area and made a new start, where God poured out His Spirit on the hungry people who attended the services.[6]

Mae Iry with Elizabeth Stieglitz (1920–1930s)

Sometime after her return to China, Elizabeth joined Mae Iry (a single lady) and her daughter and son-in-law, Robert Sonnenberg, who arrived in China in 1921. At Elizabeth's suggestion, this missionary team moved north to an unreached area of China and established a mission. For many years they held services every night, plus three services on Sundays. Large numbers turned to the Lord and destroyed their idols. Elizabeth and Mae later moved again and opened another mission, Kwo Hsien, where they worked together for several years.[7]

After Elizabeth returned from a second furlough in the mid-1920s, Mae moved to oversee the Sonnenbergs' mission when the Sonnenbergs left the field. Elizabeth remained alone at Kwo Hsien. Though China's outbursts of civil war in the 1930s made life dangerous for missionaries, Elizabeth returned for a third term in 1933. PCI Missions Director W. T. Witherspoon wrote about these single ladies in the *Pentecostal Outlook* (April 1934): "Sisters Stieglitz and Iry are enjoying a very unusual outpouring of God's Spirit in China."[8] Elizabeth (known as Stiegie to missionaries) shared the following report in 1935:

> Twenty-five years ago today I first set foot in China. I look back and see how the Lord has showered me with blessings and led me step by step. At death's door, through trials and testing, in the dark, every way closed and not knowing which way to turn, I have stood still and seen God open doors. He has never failed. I would not want to change my place for an easier one, for I have learned to know Him better.[9]

Kathryn Hendricks and Virginia Weddle with Mae Iry and Elizabeth Stieglitz (1930–1940s)

In 1936, Mae Iry returned to China from furlough with two other young ladies—Kathryn Hendricks and Virginia Weddle. Isolated in their mission stations and without means for keeping informed of world events, these single ladies did not know about the advancing Japanese troops until warnings reached their area of China. In 1939, Kathryn returned home to Oklahoma due to tuberculosis. After Kathryn left, Mae suffered internment in a concentration camp.[10]

The British consul urged Elizabeth Stieglitz to leave. However, she chose to stay to provide safety for refugees at her mission station. Fascinating details of Elizabeth's bravery, grit, and divine protection during World War II—as written by her friend, Nona Freeman—are shared in *Profiles of Pentecostal Missionaries*. During the second year of the Japanese occupation of China, Stiegie was found non-responsive in her room from a severe stroke. Though she did recover, she hovered between life and death for two weeks.[11]

After over thirty years in China, three military police from the advancing Japanese army—which took over the town of Kwo Hsien—escorted Stiegie from her mission station in March 1942. Somewhere along the journey to Shanghai, she learned she would be exchanged for a Japanese prisoner.[12] She left Shanghai by ship on June 29, 1942. On July 22, after tedious days and nights aboard the ship, she saw a welcome sight—a ship flying an American flag. The ship docked in East Africa (Mozambique) to exchange refugees and prisoners. Stiegie sailed aboard another ship on July 28, reaching New York on August 25 after a two-day stop in Brazil.[13] Missionary Carl Hensley (China), who had returned earlier, was there to meet her and took her and the Wheelers (also missionaries) to the home of Andrew Urshan, and then to an evening church service.[14]

After Elizabeth had rested and regained her strength in the States, she was anxious to return to China. She contacted Kathryn Hendricks, who had left China in 1939 when she became ill with tuberculosis. Fully recovered, Kathryn also desired to go back to China. The two ladies made plans to return despite the war. However, government restrictions delayed their return.

Elizabeth Stieglitz and Kathryn Hendricks
(1946–1950)

While the previous accounts are from Elizabeth's earlier years in China before the United Pentecostal Church was formed, later records indicate she received support as a missionary of the UPC. Interestingly, Elizabeth Stieglitz's name appears on the official missionary lists of the PAW, the PCI, and the UPC.[15] The 1947 UPC official listing of missionaries to China includes Elizabeth Stieglitz, Kathryn Hendricks, and Mae Iry.[16]

After the end of World War II, Elizabeth returned to China with Kathryn Hendricks, sailing from San Francisco on October 18, 1946.[17] They made their home in Beijing (known as "Peking" at the time) but had to be evacuated by a Lutheran Mission plane, *The St. Paul*, due to the "ruthless Communist scourge advancing on the city."[18] They spent the Christmas holiday as guests in a Lutheran hospital. Then, on December 28, 1949, the Lutheran pilot flew Elizabeth and Kathryn to Canton, South China, a distance of 995 miles. In Canton, they oversaw the mission of Daniel and Alice Sheets while Alice returned to the States for surgery.

After a year in Canton, they had to flee again to escape the advancing Red Army. They resided in Hong Kong and became involved in a ministry of compassion to the refugees. While in Hong Kong, Elizabeth collapsed physically. After three months of therapy, Elizabeth returned to the

States in a ship's hospital bed. She arrived in California in June 1950, exactly forty years after she began her missionary career in China.[19] Her years of sacrificial service had taken their toll on her health. Longtime friends made her comfortable in a cottage in Pasadena, California. She arrived home from Hong Kong at age sixty.

The March 1970 *Global Witness* shared an update Elizabeth sent to Foreign Missions[20] in which she expressed thanks for the financial and prayer support she had received. She reported that her Parkinson's disease had worsened, limiting her ability to write and do things. She added, "One thing the Parkinson's cannot do is keep me from praying. . . . The Lord is good and gracious to me. I am looking for Him to come." Although Elizabeth also suffered from severe heart disease, God extended her life twenty-five years beyond her departure from the field.[21]

God called her home on May 7, 1975, near her eighty-sixth birthday.

As I record these stories of twentieth-century pioneers, I pray that twenty-first-century Apostolics—whether married or single—will answer God's call to reach the unreached, even in challenging areas.

Alice Kugler Sheets (PAW 1920)

Alice's name appears on the 1947 UPC missionary list alongside her husband, Daniel Sheets. However, Alice first went to South China as a single missionary. She is listed as Alice Kugler among the PAW missionaries in a 1920 *Voice in the Wilderness* publication.[22]

At the close of a holiness tent meeting in 1910, Alice received a letter with news about a Pentecostal camp meeting in Topeka, Kansas. Within three months, she had read every scriptural passage she could find on the

Holy Ghost. She desperately wanted to attend the Topeka meeting, and God miraculously provided the funds for her to attend. At midnight on the third night of services, she received the Holy Ghost. For three days she spoke in tongues (in several different languages). Some of her sayings were interpreted by people who knew the languages. One of the interpreters was Daniel Sheets, who later became her husband. As Alice magnified the Lord in tongues, Daniel interpreted when she spoke in German.[23]

During her years with the Holiness movement, Alice had felt a call to foreign missions, which she initially resisted. God confirmed the calling at the Topeka camp meeting and identified the place as China. She spent the following four years in evangelistic and obstetric training. In September 1914, she boarded a ship in Seattle, Washington, with thirteen Pentecostal missionaries and set sail for China. Following a month's stay in Hong Kong, she moved inland to a mission station in South China. On location at the mission, earnest prayers for the outpouring of God's Spirit continued almost day and night. By 4:00 AM one morning, fourteen people had received the Holy Ghost, an exciting event that initiated the outpouring of God's Spirit in inland China.[24]

Due to escalating hatred and opposition toward foreigners, Alice took a furlough and decided she should remain home. While there, she became reacquainted with Daniel Sheets, whom she had known since childhood.[25] In 1926, they married and later established a church in Phoenix, Arizona. In 1934, they were endorsed as PCI missionaries to China.[26]

After the 1945 merger, Daniel and Alice continued their ministry in China under UPC appointment. Together, they spent nearly ten years as missionaries in China. At one point during their years in China they were placed under house arrest for fifteen months. However, their missionary work continued to prosper. Following their house arrest, the Japanese confined them to a concentration camp for seven months. In 1943, the Japanese released them in exchange for POWs, and they returned to the States. In 1946, they returned to China but had to leave in 1948 due to Alice's serious illness. They pastored in Prescott, Arizona, for some years. Daniel Sheets passed away in 1965. After her husband's death, Alice remained in Prescott until she died in 1979 at the age of ninety-six.[27] Reports coming out of China indicate that the Apostolic message first planted in China by Alice Kugler and later "watered" with her husband continues to bear fruit even under communist oppression.

3

India

Women Who Introduced the Apostolic Message in India

Dorothy McCarty, Telie Dover, Ferne Scism

During the years that Elizabeth Stieglitz, Alice Kugler Sheets, and other single women were proclaiming the Apostolic message in China, single ladies were also preaching the Pentecostal message in India. Daniel Scott mentions three women who served in India under the PAW during the decades before the formation of the UPC: Dorothy McCarty;[1] C. B. Herron (1913 PAW roster); and Margaret Clark in Travancore, South India (1920 PAW roster).[2]

The work of these early missionary ladies links with the pioneering work of Missionaries Ellis and Majorie Scism, appointed to India by the UPC in 1948 and arriving there in 1949. The Scisms began their work in southern India with a group of about three hundred Pentecostal believers. These believers had been converted under the ministry of Elizabeth Simmat (PAW), who had worked under Dorothy McCarty.[3]

Dorothy McCarty (in India 1909–1947)

Dorothy McCarty, a Trinitarian Pentecostal missionary, arrived in India in 1909. Soon after her arrival, she heard and accepted the Oneness message. Thus, the history of Pentecostal missionary activity in India dates back to Dorothy McCarty. The PAW listed her as one of their missionaries in 1915[4] and reported that she was the first Jesus Name missionary in India. However, she received support from all the Oneness groups and was highly esteemed. She established a mission station and opened five outstations, an orphanage, and a day school. She shared the Apostolic message in India for thirty-six years. In the years before her death, she became feeble and almost blind. She died in India in 1947[5] at age eighty-three.[6] The Ellis Scism family arrived in India two years after her death.[7]

UPC Missions Director W. T. Stairs referred to Dorothy as "Mother McCarty," one of the grandmothers of missions. According to reports, hundreds of Hindus and Muslims from the village and neighborhood came to pay their respects at her funeral service.[8]

Telie Dover (Greer) (1947–1955)

As a young single lady, Telie Dover knew Dorothy McCarty, felt God's call to India, and was intending to go there with Dorothy in 1936. She accompanied Dorothy to New York Harbor, but had to tell her goodbye since her visa had not yet come through. Telie felt sure she would see her friend soon, but she did not make it to India until after Dorothy's death in 1947.

Anyone sensing God's call into global missions would be energized and challenged by knowing Telie Dover's fascinating story. The Scisms, who worked with her in India, shared glimpses of her personality and ministry. Thankfully, William Turner gleaned insights about Telie from interviews with Harry Scism, who at age fifteen had accompanied his parents and younger sister, Ferne, to India in 1949. Such material and a summary of her life preserved in the UPCI Order of the Faith provide this portrait of vibrant Telie Dover, who was inducted into the Order of the Faith in 2019, seventeen years after her death.

The following four paragraphs, excerpted from the UPCI Order of the Faith, summarize her birth, calling, and ministry:

> **Telie Dover Greer** (July 7, 1916–June 10, 2002)
> Inducted into UPCI Order of the Faith in 2019
>
> Telie Dover Greer was born in the Ozark Mountain village of Zion, Arkansas, on July 7, 1916. Her birth name was Roxie Artelie Dover, but the name Roxie was only known by her relatives. Telie rhymes with freely, and Telie lived freely and gave her life freely for the work of the Lord.
>
> When Telie was a baby, an elderly man named Titus knocked on the door of the Dover house and asked to pray for the baby. Titus prayed and proclaimed that the baby girl would preach the gospel all over the world. This prophecy was unbelievable to the family, yet twenty years later, Telie was an international evangelist. Her ministry took her to all fifty US states and every province of Canada. She visited over fifty countries, and many miracles and healings occurred in her meetings.
>
> When Telie was nine, she had a vision of India. In her vision, thousands of Indians were falling off a mountainside, and Telie was the only one who could save them. She knew God had called her to be a missionary to India. In 1933, Ben Green preached a one-month revival in a small Oklahoma town. Only one person received the baptism of the Holy Spirit: seventeen-year-old Telie Dover. He later said the

revival had cost him $100, but the conversion of Sister Telie was worth every penny.

Telie tried to go to India in 1936, but due to complications with her visa, she could not leave. She accompanied Mother McCarty to New York Harbor and told the veteran missionary they would soon be together in India. However, Telie did not make it to McCarty's mission until 1947. By that time, McCarty had passed away.[9]

The following biographical sketch of Telie Dover—with minor adaptations—is excerpted with the author's permission from *India to the World: The Missionary Pilgrimage of Harry E. Scism*, by William D. Turner.

Telie Dover—a young and inspiring female evangelist, conspicuously bold, bluntly outspoken, beautiful but happily un-genteel as the occasion required—was a thoroughly unceremonious Pentecostal missionary to India in the postwar years just before the arrival of the Scism family to India in 1949.

A high school beauty queen in her small town in Oklahoma, she gave her heart to the Lord at a Pentecostal church in spite of the vehement opposition of her father. Telie was willing to go anywhere, under any conditions, in order to preach the gospel. She waded through muddy streams, hiked for miles on jungle trails of the Himalayan foothills, survived the bite of a deadly poisonous viper, and once slapped a hapless young man on an overcrowded Indian train when he jostled her from behind. The fatherly Ellis Scism, traveling in the same train car, told her with appalled astonishment that the student had simply accidentally bumped her with his shoulder bag.

In response to a letter from Northeast India received in the mail at Mother McCarty's mission, Telie had unhesitatingly accepted an invitation in January 1949 (two months before the Scisms arrived in southern India) to travel almost one thousand miles to explain the Apostolic doctrine to the mountain tribal people of Northeast India. She found a newly Spirit-baptized group of over one thousand Christian evangelicals who invited her to teach them the Apostolic doctrine. Several thousand other believers were affiliated with that initial group. Her ready response opened the door to an amazing Oneness Pentecostal revival in that remote, recently primitive, and previously inaccessible area not far from the border with Burma. Two generations earlier, the Indian government had closed the area because of the danger of head hunters.

Telie was the first to bring the Apostolic message to Northeast India, but she soon turned to the kind and wise leadership of fellow Oneness missionary, Ellis Scism, who, along with Telie, became God's instrument for establishing the believers among the hill tribes. Ellis continued that leadership after Telie departed from India in 1955.[10]

Initially, Telie had been told she would have to wait for an appointment as a missionary to India by the newly established United Pentecostal Church in North America, so she had applied instead to the PAW, and was approved. After arriving in India in early 1948, she had a falling out with the soon-to-be-retired successor of Mother McCarty in northern India. Later, she worked as an independent missionary until she placed herself under the fatherly oversight of UPC Missionary Ellis Scism. His endorsement helped secure her appointment as a UPC missionary to India.

Mother McCarty, the first Oneness missionary in India, had died the year before Telie arrived at the mission station in north India, located on a tributary of the Ganges River in the state of Uttar Pradesh. The PAW missionary who succeeded Mother McCarty retired and returned to the States a month after Telie arrived. The principal of the mission school, James Morar, an educated Indian who held a master's degree and served as a civil magistrate, was effectively running the school and the mission. Recognizing his proven abilities, Telie officially transferred leadership of the PAW mission to James Morar. At the time, Telie was the only American Oneness missionary in India.

A year later, when Telie began working closely with the Scism family after they arrived in south India, James Morar also became a close friend and colleague of the Scisms and a particularly close friend to Harry Scism. James preached with powerful results in crusades in south India more than once. Harry remembers that on one occasion two thousand attended the crusade meetings, and many new believers were added to the church.[11]

James Morar's son, Sheil, would later lead a group of Oneness churches in north India numbering about eight thousand constituents.

The letter that brought Telie to Northeast India was addressed to James Morar, who had served as secretary of the mission under Mother McCarty. The letter arrived at the mission not long after Telie's arrival in India. It was from Pastor Zakamlova, a tribal leader in the Mizoram area of Northeast India. A large, Spirit-filled group of believers formerly associated with the Presbyterian mission among the tribal people was asking Mother McCarty for assistance. He explained that believers among the tribal people who had accepted the experience of the baptism of the Holy Spirit were essentially rejected by their former evangelical missionary leaders. Their churches were without official recognition and under intense pressure from both the government and former missionary leaders to disband. They needed help. Telie wrote back to tell the leader that Mother McCarty had recently died, but Telie, as a PAW missionary, would come and offer her help.[12]

Telie traveled with an interpreter one thousand miles north to Assam State in Northeast India, where she would meet with church leaders of the southernmost Mizo tribe located in the Lushai Hills area. The elevation increased as she traveled into the heavy forests of the tribal region. As her train crossed into Northeast India, it was quickly apparent that she was moving into a region of the Indian subcontinent more closely related in language and culture to southeast Asia, such as the nations of Burma and Thailand, rather than the South Asian languages and religions of the lower Indian subcontinent.[13]

Telie was warmly received by the churches and pastors under Pastor Zakamlova's leadership. After listening to her teaching on Apostolic doctrine, about one thousand believers were ready to be baptized in the name of Jesus Christ. Telie baptized only Zakamlova, and he in turn organized the baptism of the first one thousand Mizo tribesmen in Jesus' name. She assisted the leaders in preparing an initial church constitution and helped them obtain legal status with the government. . . .

Soon after their arrival in southern India, Ellis Scism, traveling with an interpreter, made his first trip to the Lushai Hills in February 1950. . . . Telie joined them on the last leg of the trip by train and Jeep. Meeting with Pastor Zakamlova and other church leaders, Telie encouraged the group to become part of the worldwide fellowship of the United Pentecostal Church. They did, and Zakamlova became the first ordained minister of the UPC in Northeast India. Ellis Scism would visit the churches in Northeast India annually thereafter to teach, provide administrative oversight, conduct conferences and seminars, and license and ordain a growing cadre of national leaders. Government travel restrictions made more frequent visits impossible.

Telie, faced with visa restrictions in India, ended her missionary work there in 1955. However, she had made critical contributions in establishing the Oneness message in India, particularly as the first to bring the Apostolic message to Northeast India.[14]

The citation for Telie Dover Greer's induction into the UPCI Order of the Faith gives further details of Telie's life.

In 1956, when Telie was forty years old, she married Talmadge Greer, and they returned to India. Their first son, Landis, was born in 1957. The baby's health required them to return to the United States, but Sister Telie continued to pray for her "beloved India." The couple later served as missionaries in Central America, and Telie continued to travel and minister until she was in her eighties. She passed from this life on June 10, 2002.[15]

About a month before Telie died, she wrote a letter of encouragement to her family.

> I have survived much in my life . . . rejection and obstacles, thieves with machetes, being caught on fire, nearly drowning, terrorism and revolution, being bitten by India's deadliest snake, hunger, famine, drought, heat, and hardship. I survived to tell you to *press on*. Preacher, preach on! Singer, sing on! Teacher, teach on! Soulwinner, win on!
>
> Never give up! Never forget the power in His name! It is the only name. Never forget the power of His Spirit! It is the only Spirit. Never forget the power of godliness! It is the only way. And please, never forget the power of endurance. It is what wins the race! Endure to the end. Finish strong! I love you.[16]

Ferne Scism (Ackley)

(Assistant Missionary, June 1953–July 1965)

Ferne arrived in India in May 1949 with her parents, Ellis and Marjorie Scism, and brother, Harry. Ferne was thirteen when she began missionary life in India. Four years later, in June 1953, she received her personal appointment to India as an assistant missionary. She resigned in July 1965.[17] Then, in June 1975, the Foreign Missions Board recommended Ferne as a missionary associate to India.[18]

Appointed in 1948, the Scism family boarded a ship in Portland, Oregon, with a stop in Seattle, Washington, on their voyage to India. As friends of the Scisms, my parents, Alvin and Tressa Kantola, traveled to Oregon from Idaho to bid them farewell. Not long before boarding their ship, Ferne discovered that her accordion needed repair. Learning that the repairs could be done during their Seattle stop, my parents drove to Seattle to provide transportation for the Scisms to the repair shop.

During her years in India with her parents and as a student in boarding school, Ferne actively participated in their missionary work. In 1955, Ferne returned to the States for one year and attended Conquerors Bible College, where I also attended. Her enthusiastic sharing of missionary experiences impacted us students during that year. Her vibrant piano playing and fascinating stories are pleasant memories for those who shared the 1955–56 school year with her. Time spent with Ferne always added a note of joy and excitement about life and serving the Lord.

In *India to the World*, Ferne's brother, Harry, commented that Ferne's love for the people of India and her intense burden for the millions of unreached people on this great subcontinent kept her in India for fourteen years. A serious health problem necessitated that she leave India and return to the States. Harry described his sister as "a very consecrated child of God." Back in the US, Ferne began traveling as her anointed preaching and musical talent opened many doors for her. One of Ferne's favorite songs, which depicted her love for God, was "Take Everything but My Lord."[19]

Her single years ended in 1981, when she married Joseph Ackley. Joe and Ferne made their home in Oregon. Joe passed away in 2009, and Ferne lived another ten years until October 25, 2019. In her last years, Ferne lived at Harvest Homes in Portland, a facility established by her late uncle, Ernest Moyer, also the founding president of Conquerors Bible College in Portland.

4

East Asia (Japan and South Korea)

May Heath (Gray), Frances Munsey, Ey Ja Kim

Japan

May Heath (Gray), before 1906

At the dawn of the twentieth century, even before God began pouring out His Spirit at the Azusa Street Mission in Los Angeles, a single lady felt a definite call to Japan. She obeyed the call and went. Back in the States some years later, she received the Holy Ghost and returned to Japan as a married lady. She became known as the "Mother of Pentecost in Japan."

While the name of this young lady, May Heath, would not be recognized as an appointed missionary of the UPCI, many Apostolic believers are familiar with the name of her grandson, Kenneth Haney, who served as general superintendent of the UPCI from 2000 to 2008. Others might know of May's daughter, Olive Haney, the mother of Kenneth Haney and wife of Clyde Haney, founding president of Western Apostolic Bible College (now Christian Life College) in Stockton, California. While some would have heard about Frank and May Gray, who served as self-supporting missionaries in Japan, they likely would not know that May went to Japan in 1902 as a single lady at age twenty-five.

Olive Haney describes her mother's call to Japan in *Profiles of Pentecostal Missionaries.*[1] When young May told her father about her calling, he felt troubled and said to her, "Oh, May, I cannot bear to give you up. Our family would be too lonely and bereft. You know we have already lost two of our dear children."[2] May, born in 1877, was the oldest of eight children. Though May did not want to leave her family, her love for God and burden for Japan persisted.

May graduated from high school in 1893, attended a teacher's college, and became a kindergarten teacher. At about twenty-one years of age, she began volunteer work in the slums of Philadelphia. She did this work without remuneration, yet God provided for her needs. In 1900, she felt the need for more Bible training and enrolled in a Missionary Alliance school founded by the well-known Dr. A. B. Simpson, "a man strong on faith, healing, sanctification, and the missionary cause."[3]

With her burden for Japan beckoning, May left her home in Pennsylvania accompanied by her friend, Pearlie Ague. They traveled by train to San Francisco and then by boat to Japan. Though deathly seasick for three weeks, May remained full of zeal to do the will of God. Reaching Hiroshima, she studied the customs and language. From there, she went to Kobe and opened a prison work. She also ministered in Tokyo and traveled into the interior, where many people had never seen a white woman. May observed that the people worshiped gods of fear. Even while learning the language, May preached and taught them about the God of love who became flesh and gave His life for them. "One day at the close of her message, a Japanese individual approached her, asking, 'Where can I get some of this Jesus soap?' In speaking of the blood of Jesus that washes whiter than snow, she had used a wrong word, giving the impression that 'Jesus soap' would make one's skin white."[4]

May's strenuous and wholehearted work took a toll on her health, and a doctor ordered her to return to the United States. Before leaving Japan, she received a tract in the mail telling about the outpouring of the Holy Ghost at the Azusa Mission in Los Angeles. Reading the tract gave her a hunger for the infilling of the Spirit and a desire to visit California to know more. After returning to Pennsylvania, a doctor recommended that she move to a milder climate (like California) for her health. Her mother accompanied her to Redlands, California. May searched for the mission on Azusa Street and learned that the group had disbanded. Though she felt disappointed, God had a plan. A salesman showed up at their door. Rather than trying to sell them horseradish, he told May and her mother about the Holy Ghost. As he stood on their doorstep, he began to worship God and soon burst forth speaking in tongues. He directed them to a nearby Pentecostal church. May attended the church and later received the Holy Ghost. May did not think it wise to return to Japan as a single lady because of her hard experiences there.

In 1906, the year May returned to America from Japan, a young man from Washington State graduated from Nyack Bible Institute in New York. He moved to California and began to attend the Pentecostal Church in Pomona, even though he was a "hard-shell Baptist." There he met May and felt attracted to her. In time, he proposed. May asked for time to pray, wanting to be sure of God's will and that she truly loved him. In a church service, she felt God give her an overwhelming love for Frank Gray.

Frank and May married on January 4, 1910. In 1914, they sailed to Japan to take the Holy Ghost message to the Japanese. Though May had received the Holy Ghost, Frank did not receive the Spirit until 1920. In Japan, they heard and believed the message of the oneness of God and Jesus Name baptism. Frank found another missionary to baptize him in Jesus' name. When the Upper Room Mission, which supported them, heard of their acceptance of water baptism in Jesus' name, they withdrew their support. The Grays stayed in Japan and lived by faith, trusting God for their needs. God used George B. Studd, a Oneness believer who collected and sent money to missionaries as he felt directed, to meet some of the Grays' needs. The Grays also taught English to professional people as a means of making a living. Many people they taught received baptism in Jesus' name and the infilling of the Spirit.

The combination of May Heath Gray's single and married missionary years earned her the title of the "Mother of Pentecost in Japan."[5] Frank Gray suffered a stroke between 1946 and 1948, which left him with mental and physical impairment. When they returned to the States, May kept constant letter-writing contact with the Japanese believers. After May died in 1954 at the age of seventy-seven, Frank continued to receive letters from the Japanese. Though the Grays did not serve as UPC-appointed missionaries, their faith, fellowship, and family legacy linked them securely with the UPCI through their daughter Olive, who became an influential leader in the UPCI as the wife of Clyde Haney. Also, their son David Gray founded and pastored a strong missions-supporting church in San Diego, California.

Frances Munsey (June 1970 to September 1978)

Frances Munsey served in Japan for eight years under appointment with the UPCI. However, her missionary life began in 1963 and extended beyond 1978. She obeyed God's call to Japan as a single lady in her midthirties.

When searching for material to write Frances's story, I learned about her younger brother, Darrel, and contacted him. I was pleasantly surprised when he told me that Frances had written her story and that he would be happy to send me a copy. Selected content from her unpublished booklet, "Only One Life," provides a vivid view of serving in missions in earlier decades when missionaries traveled by ship and lived with limited resources.[6]

Frances grew up in Tulsa, Oklahoma, as one of four children. Her mother was a devout Christian who kept the children in church even though her father did not care for church or the Christian life. During her childhood, Frances repeatedly read the words on a plaque in the family living room: "Only one life will soon be past; only what is done for Christ will last." She dedicated her life to Christ in her early teen years when she received the baptism of the Holy Ghost and knew she would someday become a missionary.

After finishing high school in 1951, Frances wanted to attend Bible college but found it impossible. When an invitation came from her older brother, Frank, to move to Oshkosh, Wisconsin, to help in his church, she happily moved there. She found an office job and assisted in the small church. When Frank moved to Hammond, Indiana, to pioneer a church, she moved and worked there. From time to time, she returned to Tulsa and did office work. Feeling God's call, she spent time studying the Bible and was finally able to attend Apostolic College in Tulsa. She also completed several Moody Bible Institute Mastery Bible Courses.

In 1958, Frances's father was killed in an auto accident. At that time, Frances's family was living in Indiana and she was living in Tulsa, working in the office of the T. L. Osborn Evangelistic Association, where she learned about overseas missions work. Her father's death brought changes. Her mother and eleven-year-old Darrel returned to Tulsa, and the three lived together, providing a secure homelife for her brother. At some point, Frances began working at St. John's Hospital in Tulsa as an accounts payable clerk and bookkeeping machine operator. During her three years on this job, she continued to feel God's tug and diligently prayed for His direction. She had always loved the Far East and sensed God's call might be to China, Korea, or Japan.

She became very sick during the winter of 1962 but continued to work. Finally, her illness confined her to bed. During this time, God showed her a vision of her life if she denied God's call and remained in Tulsa. She awoke from that vision or dream crying out, "God, please let me go and work for You!"

At the same time, God spoke to Eva, her mother: "Frances must go and become a missionary. If you hinder her, then her life will be taken." Eva responded, "No, don't take my daughter, Lord. She must go and work for You." After Eva prayed, Frances began to improve, and her strength returned. As it turned out, Eva joined Frances on the mission field in Japan and stayed for over eighteen years.

In the summer of 1962, Frances's pastor's wife, Mary Williams, called her and told her that Leonard Coote, who operated Ikoma Bible College in Nara, Japan, was looking for someone to work in the college office. Mary thought Frances could fill the need. Leonard had been working in

Japan for about fifty years at that time and had established Ikoma Bible College. During World War II, while Leonard was in the States, he had founded the International Bible College in San Antonio, Texas. Leonard Coote met with Frances in Tulsa, and plans were made for Frances to travel to Japan in May 1963 with John Bell and his wife. Leonard also advised Frances to travel to San Antonio to visit the Bible college. While in San Antonio, she met and talked with the Bells, who shared the good and bad aspects of living in Japan.

On April 19, 1963, Frances said goodbye to her friends at St. John's Hospital and her church. With household items crated and personal goods packed in trunks, she shipped them to California to be loaded on the ship she would board. She then traveled to Chicago by train for a weeklong visit with her brother, Frank Munsey, and his family. The Evangelistic Temple of Hammond, Indiana, which Frank pastored, supported her during all her missionary years in Japan. From Indiana, she flew to Long Beach, California, where she boarded an American President Lines passenger ship for transit to Japan.

Frances vividly described her departure. She boarded the ship and located her room on the lower deck. The room had two bunk beds. She and the Davises, who had come aboard to help her get situated, then looked for the Bell family and another family scheduled to travel with her. Not finding them, the Davises finally had to leave. Frances stayed on deck, watching for the two couples. She was "so happy to see them" when they finally arrived. They all stayed on deck to watch the ship sail away from the dock at midnight on a clear night. They continued to watch as the shoreline became smaller and smaller.

Frances wrote that she felt such peace and calm knowing she was going in God's perfect will.

During their two weeks aboard the ship, John Bell organized a Japanese language class for daily study. John had spent time in Japan, and his wife had been born and raised there. When the ship stopped for a day in Honolulu, the group rented a car to see the sights of Hawaii and visit with a missionary. Again, the ship sailed at midnight. At last, early one morning, the ship sailed into Yokohama, Japan, and beautiful Mount Fuji appeared on the horizon.

Missionary June Nukida and other missionaries welcomed the new arrivals. Left-driving traffic and the Japanese restaurant menu were "foreign" experiences to Frances, followed by boarding the train among the rushing and pushing people. It was the beginning of her habit of running and hurrying to get anywhere in Japan.

Frances was happy and excited upon arriving at the Ikoma Bible College. The campus sat amid mountains with majestic Mount Ikoma as a backdrop. The scenic area had not been bombed during World War II. Soon after their arrival, Leonard Coote served them a big dinner and then showed Frances her four-room house on the side of the mountain. She loved the view from the kitchen window, which overlooked the campus. She smiled upon entering the western-style bathroom with a large tub and toilet. However, her smile vanished when she discovered the toilet had no plumbing; water had to be poured into the toilet bowl to flush it. The single faucet in the bathroom sink provided only cold water for the sink, tub, and toilet. Warm baths involved building a fire outside and waiting an hour for water to heat. Frances was reassured when she learned that a Japanese student would fix her bath three times each week.

The day after she arrived at the school, Leonard took her on a tour of the campus—four large buildings and about eight homes. On the tour, she met Ruth Boring, who would be leaving in a few months, and the Kanau family scheduled to leave the next month for furlough. Knowing that the Bell family would be living in Kobe, she suddenly realized she would be the only American missionary on the campus. Leonard would be gone most of the time overseeing the Bible schools in Korea and Texas.

Ruth Boring introduced her to the churches in the area. On Sunday morning they attended the Osaka church, and in the evening they went to Ishikiri church, not far from Ikoma. The Ishikiri church became Frances's home church during all her years in Japan. On her first Monday in Japan, Frances began language study with Okada Sensei, a lady who had taught Japanese to the missionaries for many years. The Sensei family had lost everything they owned during World War II and had moved into a house on the Ikoma Bible College campus with their three children. When Leonard Coote returned after the war, he found them there. Okada was a Christian, but her husband was not. Unexpectedly, he got baptized one Sunday morning when he took his children to Sunday school. Soon after, he became very sick, and the following day he died. Leonard hired Okada to teach missionaries Japanese and to work in the school office. In later years, she became pastor of the Ishikiri church.

For the next two years, Frances studied Japanese every morning from 8:00 to 9:00 AM and worked in the office until 5:00 PM. She kept a very scheduled life with office work and helping in the Ishikiri church. Frances wrote that Leonard Coote was very disciplined, having been a businessman in England before becoming a missionary, and he expected a lot out of her. He had shown her the bank business and church locations one time and thereafter expected her to function on her own. Frances soon began teaching the English Bible classes on Sunday formerly taught by Ruth Boring. She also started a Wednesday evening Bible class. Frances wrote, "Through these Bible classes, I was able to see some young Japanese students receive Christ in their hearts and receive baptism."

In 1965, Frances moved to Tokyo to study advanced Japanese and to work with the missionaries there. She lived in a one-room apartment and slept on the floor. While living there, she began planning to launch into pioneer missionary work. With advice from her former language teacher, Okada Sensei, Frances invited Yayoi, a young Japanese lady and recent college graduate, to join her in her pioneer work. She told Yayoi that she had little money and was living by faith. She promised to share what she had and always provide a home. Because Yayoi came to work with her by faith, she began calling her Faith. The two women helped the missionary in Tokyo for a time, then God opened a door for them to move back to the Osaka area. They opened their first church in Itami City, the location of the Osaka International Airport.

They rented a duplex within a ten-minute ride of the train station and started teaching English to a friendly group of students in a rented room in the city hall. They held church services in their duplex and rented a small hall nearby for children's services. During their first month in Itami City, they faced a financial crisis when a check they had received was canceled. On the day they needed replacement money they received a special-delivery letter from missionaries in Tokyo, saying God had told them to send money immediately. God had met Faith and Frances's need right on time!

Frances worked at a language school in Nishinomiya as one source of income. One day the owner (a Japanese missionary married to an American) asked Frances to begin teaching the English Bible class with the stipulation that she couldn't teach about miracles, for those days had passed. She needed the job, but felt she could not continue teaching with that kind of limitation. Discouraged, Frances and Faith were trudging home from the train station when they heard a man whistling the song "Launch Out into the Deep." They followed him for a distance trying to catch up, but he always remained out of reach. When they rounded the corner that led to their duplex, he had disappeared. They both felt God had sent an angel to encourage them at that moment. The following week Frances found a job as an English teacher at the National Electric Company in Osaka. She worked there for several years.

A heavy rain was pelting the ground one Sunday evening, causing Frances and Faith to doubt anyone would attend their English Bible class. Through the rain they spotted two high school boys lounging on a nearby porch. Frances called out to them and invited them to the class. Surprisingly, they came. They soon became constant visitors and believers. After their baptisms, they became faithful helpers. One they called Sketch, as his Japanese name was hard to remember, and the other one they named Mike.

Around this time, Eva, Frances's mother, came to visit, having felt for some time that Frances needed her. This meant they needed a bigger house, but finding one proved difficult. As it turned out, they finally found a home in nearby Takarazuka, where they held Bible studies and continued to travel to Itami three or four times a week for services. In the summer of 1966, Frances arranged for Faith to travel to America and attend Apostolic Bible Institute in St. Paul, Minnesota. Faith made straight A's while working part-time. With Faith gone, Frances went back to language school twice a week, and Sketch and Mike helped with the church. They baptized around fifteen converts during their first two years in Itami.

Frances and her mother took their first furlough in 1967. Another missionary took over their work for four months. While Frances was in America, Eva obtained a missionary visa and returned to Japan with Frances in August 1967. The mother-daughter team continued the work in Itami as well as starting an additional work in Takarazuka. They later moved from their apartment in Itami City to a large house in Takarazuka. Before Faith's departure to America, they had placed a gospel tract in every house in Itami City. Frances and her mother continued distributing tracts, traveling by bus to the rural areas. They walked miles and miles through rice fields to place tracts in clusters of houses.

During those early years as an independent missionary, Frances had worked cooperatively with UPC missionaries in Japan. She eventually was invited to become a part of the UPC missions team in that nation. She sent her application to the UPC Foreign Missions Board, and was duly appointed as a minister and missionary. Financial support was delayed until she could return to the States for deputation.

As an appointed UPC missionary, Frances asked the UPC Bible college in Kyoto for assistance in finding a qualified pastor for the growing congregation of the

Takarazuka church. Two weeks later, a Bible college graduate inquired about the church. He was a tall, handsome Chinese man named So, who had grown up in Japan. Frances felt impressed that he would be the perfect pastor for Takarazuka. She located a room for him in the city, and he started helping her with the church.

At the end of 1969, she returned to the United States with her mother to meet the missionary board. At the 1970 General Conference in Portland, Oregon, she was commissioned as a missionary to Japan.

On their arrival back in Japan, Frances and Eva were pleased to see the excellent work done by Pastor So. With the Takarazuka church under capable leadership, Francis made plans to start a church in another city. A real estate friend helped them locate a lovely house in the mountain city of Kawanishi, about thirty minutes from Takarazuka and Itami. They put up a sign calling their house “Kawanishi Christian Center.” As an appointed missionary of the UPCI, Frances now had the resources to advance the work. She purchased their first telephone, bought a new Toyota, and mounted speakers on the top to announce church services. As she drove through the streets of the cities, she recalled having walked those same streets for many years. Frances and her mother lived and worked in Kawanishi City from 1970 to 1978.

The mountain city of Kawanishi was cold and snowy in the winter. Itami and Takarazuka, only short distances away, had no snow. From the beginning of their church in Kawanishi, many children attended their Sunday school, with an average of one hundred each Sunday. Then high school and college students began attending, and many young people gave their hearts to God. When Frances began preparing for furlough in 1978, Pastor So suggested combining the three churches in the Kawanishi City building. The distance between cities was close.

When Frances returned to America for her next furlough, she met the missionary board at the General Conference and realized that the status of the work in Japan was changing. Six months later, the UPCI closed its mission in Japan and turned all the churches over to the United Pentecostal Church of Japan (JUPC). The JUPC felt no need for missionaries at that time, although eventually fully appointed and short-term missionaries would be welcomed by the Japanese church.

In the following years, Frances and her mother lived and worked in both America and Japan. In April 1987, they moved to Bryan, Texas, where Frances began working at Texas A&M University. There she began teaching a University Plus class in Japanese. After twenty-three years of missionary work in Japan, she was well-qualified to teach the language and the culture.

Her employment with Texas A&M eventually led her back to Japan. Texas A&M opened a campus in Koriyama, Japan, and she was hired as a secretary. She worked there from August 1990 to August 1991 and attended the Hosonuma church, where she preached occasionally and taught English conversation classes. Though she returned to College Station in Texas in 1991, her heart remained in Japan.

Frances's mother, Eva Lean Munsey, who had worked alongside her daughter for many years in Japan, lived to the age of ninety-four and passed away on April 23, 2004. Frances entered her heavenly abode at age seventy-five, four years later (January 21, 2008). The impact of her missionary work continues through the ministry of the

Japanese people, many of whom were converted to truth under Frances's ministry.

South Korea

Ey Ja Kim (1985–Active)

Ey Ja Kim began missionary work in South Korea as an AIMer in 1985. In 1991, she advanced to a career missionary appointment. As of the time of this writing, she has started three new churches, has helped to start two churches, and has trained over twenty-two young men and women to minister the gospel. Those ministers pastor churches or serve as assistant pastors. Three of the students have started new churches, which they now pastor. Missionary Kim has served as the interpreter for all of South Korea's camp meetings, seminars, and general conferences. All seventeen members of her family in South Korea have been won to the Lord through her influence.

Ey Ja conducts pastors-and-wives seminars to unite the Korean brethren. She serves as a General Board member of the UPCK, a member of the Board of Trustees, and the Bible school president. She also works with the Filipino UPC church in Seoul and preaches for them once a month. A new Filipino church is being started in the city of Hwasun. She is working to strengthen the Bible school so more students can be trained for Apostolic ministry in Korea.

When asked to share her missionary story, she kindly responded with her testimony, prefacing her story with two verses of Scripture: "For there is no respect of persons with God" (Romans 2:11). "But by the grace of God I am what I am: and his grace which was bestowed upon me was not in vain" (I Corinthians 15:10). Then she added, "It is my honor and privilege to share my testimony to glorify the wonderful name of Jesus!" She interspersed her story with Bible verses as follows:

> I would like to take this amazing opportunity to express my sincere appreciation and thankfulness to Global Missions for highlighting single women missionaries during the seventy-nine years of our UPCI history. "Rejoice evermore. Pray without ceasing. In everything give thanks: for this is the will of God in Christ Jesus concerning you" (I Thessalonians 5:16–18).
>
> I was born in Nam Hae, South Korea, a very small island in the far South. My father and the rest of my family were a mix of the religions of Buddhism, Confucianism, and superstition. But I was not any of those; I was an atheist. My father attended a university in Japan and was a professor at Kookmin University in Pusan, South Korea. My oldest brother, Joe, was sent to the States to study through Yonsei University in the 1950s to study at the state's expense. My father wanted me to be a medical doctor and sent me to the States to attend a university when I was twenty years old. I went with my elder brother, Peter. I wasn't happy to leave Korea because I was going to a foreign country not knowing the language.
>
> In America, I spent my first year studying English at an institute that teaches English to foreign students. I then took a college entrance examination and was accepted into a college on a probational basis. If I didn't pass the first semester, then I would be dismissed. I realized I could never

become a doctor because the subject matter was too difficult to remember, especially the vocabulary. After about three semesters, I changed my major to business administration with a minor in accounting, which was much easier for me to study. After I graduated, I worked at Arthur Andersen & Co. in their Washington, D.C. office. This company was the world's largest accounting firm at the time. I worked for this firm for fifteen years.

I had planned my future. I was quite determined about where I wanted my career to go, how rich I was going to be, where I was going, and when and where I wanted to retire. I was very worldly and had no inkling of life after death. I thought that when a person died, that was the end of everything. For that reason I enjoyed life the best way I knew how, thinking there were no consequences. I would take long vacations each year, going to Bermuda, the Bahamas, London, Paris, Hawaii, Costa del Sol, and other places. I would spend what I earned mostly on vacations, clothes, makeup, and disco dancing. However, I never drank or smoked, for which I thank God!

The accounting firm I worked for, with the partners, managers, and office workers, totaled about 1,500 employees. I was supervising an accounting department and making very good money. A young Korean lady transferred in from our company's New York office to work on a word processor. When she found out there was a Korean lady in our office, we became friends. She had been a Roman Catholic until a Pentecostal coworker witnessed to her. She talked to me about Jesus every day when we met for lunch. The daily conversations about Jesus bothered me. I finally told her that during the next five years, after I'd had a chance to have a good time in the world, I *might* go to church with her. About three years later (1982), she announced that her church was having a revival service and invited me to come. Knowing the kind of person I was, she told me the young preacher had red hair and was very handsome. I opened my mouth to say no, but my mouth said, "Yes, I will go with you."

I had no choice but to go with her since my mouth had said yes. I visited the UPC in Arlington, Virginia, making up my mind beforehand that I would never go again. If my friend asked me again to go to church, I planned to tell her, "I already went with you. Once is enough."

At the first evening's service, Evangelist Mike Meadows from Grove City, Ohio, was preaching. I didn't understand much of what he said, but I was crying out so loudly that he couldn't preach! He finally told the congregation he was going to stop preaching since God was already working. I was still crying when Mike Meadows came over to me and told me I could be baptized that night since I had repented of my sins. I told him, "I'm a sinner. I don't know anything about Jesus or the church. So how could I be qualified to be baptized?" He replied, "You are qualified to be baptized because you have repented of your sins." I said, "If that's the case, then please do so." I was baptized in the name of Jesus for the remission of my sins. The next night, I received the Holy Ghost, the precious gift from the Lord. That was my turning point. As I remember, the revival services lasted a long time. Many people came into the church from the street, and we had the biggest revival in Arlington up to that time.

When Jesus found me, the energy I had spent on the world was transferred to the Lord, the worship services, and obeying whatever my pastor was teaching from the pulpit. I was so happy I didn't know what to do! I even forgot to get married!

Soon after I was born again of the water and the Spirit, I found out I had cancer. My longtime boyfriend, a tax lawyer, was working at the same office. I wanted to marry him—until I found out he was already married! So after I was born again, the first thing I did was break up with my boyfriend. I didn't want to keep sinning again and again, so I made up my mind to stop seeing him. He said I was crazy and asked to see me one last time. I saw him "one last time" and committed the same sin again. I then knew why I had got sick; God was teaching me a good and wonderful lesson. That truly was the last time I saw the man. I asked God to forgive me and told Him that I would not commit the same sin again. I went to the altar every Sunday and Wednesday, asking the Lord to forgive me and heal me of cancer.

I told my pastor about the sin, and for nine months I kept asking him to lay his hand on my head and pray for me. Out of desperation, I promised God that if He would heal me, I would do anything He wanted me to do. After nine months, on a Sunday morning, I was at the altar praying when the Lord spoke to my heart that I was healed. On Monday I went to my doctor, who told me it was a miracle; I was whole and clean. No cancer! *God had healed me!*

God had a plan in delaying my healing for nine months. During those nine months, I learned how to pray, how to be obedient to the Word of God, how not to forsake the assembling of ourselves together, how good our God is, and much more. And, of course, I kept my promise to Him.

Since arriving in the States in 1963, I had never returned to Korea. America was so good that I had no desire to return to my homeland. However, after I was born again, the Lord spoke to me through the Word of God to go back to Korea: "But ye shall receive power, after that the Holy Ghost is come upon you: and ye shall be witnesses unto me both in Jerusalem, and in all Judaea, and in Samaria, and unto the uttermost part of the earth" (Acts 1:8).

The Lord called me the year following my salvation. For the first time since I had moved to the States, I desired to visit my dad, whom I had not seen for twenty years. I suddenly realized I needed to visit Korea and tell my dad about this wonderful Jesus. So I made an eventful visit back to my homeland. When I arrived, my father was so surprised that he asked, "Why did you come?" After I explained why I had come, he told me there was no need for me to stay because he had no desire to change his religion from Buddhism to Christianity. He told me to stay one week, rest, and then go back to my job in the States so I could earn money and send some to him.

But I disobeyed my dad because I had taken a year-long leave of absence from my job. I ended up staying with him for a year. I started telling my whole family about Jesus, my Savior. My mother had passed away the year before I went to the States, and my dad had remarried. I had a stepmother, a stepbrother, and two stepsisters whom I had never seen. I prayed three times every day in the room where my family had ancestor worship. Every day I rebuked that spirit of ancestor worship in my father's house. I asked my dad to burn all his books on the occult. He burned them all before he was born again of water and of the Holy Spirit. That was a miracle in itself. Praise the Lord!

In a two-month period, my whole family got baptized in Jesus' name for the remission of their sins, and they all received the gift of the Holy Ghost! My whole family started to witness and bring people to my father's home for services. Every Sunday, my small room was filled with people, and in turn, they also were baptized. I didn't know much about the Word of God at that time, but I did know about baptism, so I told them to be baptized to wash away their sin. After the year was almost over and it was time for me to return to my job, over twenty people had been baptized in Jesus' name and filled with the Holy Ghost!

Because I needed to leave and return to my job, I realized that these people needed a church and a pastor. The Lord spoke to me to build a church for these people. I told the Lord, "I don't have the money to build a church." He reminded me that the Lord had given me a good job in Washington, D.C. So I called my boss, Fred Weir, and asked him to send me my retirement money. Fred told me he could not send that money unless he terminated my job. I replied, "Then terminate me and send me the money." After I received the funds, I discovered it was the perfect amount to build the church. My stepmother gave me the land on which to build the church. When we dedicated the Nam Hae UPC church unto the Lord, we were not one penny in debt. And the UPCK headquarters sent a pastor for this church.

We, as humans, plan our futures. But the Bible says God is the one who leads us. I am so glad He is leading me! I am so happy that I am His servant, and He is my Leader, my Strength, my Savior, my Rock, and my all.

After the church was built in Korea, I returned to the States and went to see my former boss to tell him how much I appreciated him sending me my retirement money. With a big smile, he asked me to come back to work after one week of rest. I worked for him for three more years before my full appointment as a missionary.

After my first deputation, I returned to Korea and, with the help of God, started the second new work in the city of Changwon near an elementary school. I stayed there for four years, and we had a big revival. Every Saturday I went out to witness and soon had over thirty people in the church.

After my second deputation, with the help of God again, the third new work was started in the city of Okpo. While I was still working in Okpo, I attended our UPCK General Conference in 2000 and was elected president of the Bible school here in Korea. They have continued to reelect me for the last twenty-two years. I oversee our Filipino church in Seoul. We have over twenty saints in the church who have jobs in South Korea. They are precious saints of God.

Pastor D. G. Hargrove of Garland, Texas, preached at our Family Camp Meeting. After the camp meeting, he told me, "I will put you in charge of starting a new church in Korea from my church in Texas." I was his interpreter for the camp. We started a church in Seoul, South Korea, the funds for which were supplied by his church. They supported the church for two whole years until it became self-supporting. The church is doing very well under the leadership of Pastor Sung Hwa Seh.

The Lord raised up twelve disciples and commissioned them to reach the whole world. In the spring semester (2022), I had seventeen students enrolled and studying online. Thirty-five students have graduated so far. I am the Lord's obedient servant doing the best I know how. Please pray for our Bible school that God will send many young men and women who desire to do the work of the Lord. Of the graduates, sixteen are pastoring churches, and six have started a new church each in Daegu, Seoul, Kyong Ju, Young San, Mokpo, and Anyang. The other graduates are helping and assisting pastors. People are being born again, and sinners are being added to the kingdom of God because of the Bible school training.

When I first returned to Korea in 1985, this country was a man's world. I didn't see any women ministers, nor did they recognize women in ministry. God knew that, so He performed two miracles in my life soon after I arrived in Korea. A grandmother who lived next door to my father's home told people she was going to destroy our red brick church with an ax. When my dad told me about it, I visited her and started witnessing to her. I told her how blessed she was because I had come from America to Korea and brought her some wonderful news. She asked what the news was. I started to tell her about Jesus, and she agreed to come to church the following Sunday.

The next day, while I was washing my clothes in a puddle (in those days there were no washing machines), the Lord told me to "stand and see." When I stood, I saw people walking in one direction, so I followed them. They went to the grandmother's home I had visited the day before. On the threshing floor of her home, people were crying loudly. I asked them why, and they told me the grandmother had committed suicide because her three grandchildren in Seoul had died the night before due to a gas leak in their room. She thought her son might kill himself because of this tragedy, and she didn't want to see that, so she killed herself by drinking a whole bottle of pesticide.

I asked where her body was lying and was told she was in a room in the lower part of the house. I asked them to move her body to the upper room where I had witnessed to her. After she was brought to the upper room, I entered the room, allowing only the grandmother's daughter to come in with me. I knelt and asked the Lord to forgive the grandmother because she hadn't known that killing herself was a sin. I also told the Lord she was willing to come to church and that she needed to be born again. If she died now, she would go to Hell. I asked the Lord to have mercy on her. Then I laid my hand on her forehead and prayed in Jesus' name, commanding her life to come back. She vomited up all the poison, and after a while, she sat up and told me God was good!

What happened to the people who were crying outside for her? That miracle brought a revival to our church! When fellow ministers heard about the miracle, they were very respectful to me. This miracle took care of all the hindrances I might have had as a single woman in ministry. Glory to God!

The second miracle was that our general superintendent, Pastor Chin, invited all our ministers to his church to hear my testimony. While I was sharing my testimony about God performing miracles, God healed many of the ministers who were sick. Glory to Jesus! The Bible tells us in I Corinthians 1:26–29, "For ye see your calling, brethren, how that not many wise men after the flesh, not many mighty, not many noble, are called: but God hath chosen the foolish things of the world to confound the wise; and God hath chosen the weak things of the world to confound the things which are mighty . . . that no flesh should glory in his presence." These two miracles made a way for me to be able to minister in Korea with our brethren and with their respect. "For there is no respect of persons with God" (Romans 2:11). He can do all things! To God be the glory! We serve a wonderful God who answers our prayers.

> S. G. Lee, who has a good business, has been a tremendous help with our Bible school finances for the last twenty years. As president of our Bible school for twenty-two years, I consider that a big miracle. Other General Board members are usually elected for one or two terms, but God has granted me His favor for the last twenty-two years to keep me in our Bible school. I praise the Lord for His goodness, mercy, and grace.
>
> May the Lord richly bless you all in His wonderful name—Jesus!
>
> – Sister E. J. Kim, Missionary to South Korea

Elizabeth Turner, with her husband, William, served in South Korea as missionaries. The following is Elizabeth's memory of other events relating to Missionary E. J. Kim.

I remember Missionary Kim's account of how she won her stepmother. It was rice-planting time when Ey Ja Kim arrived back in Korea, so day after day she went to the flooded fields in her skirts, blouses, and tights (to repel the leeches), and worked alongside her stepmother. When Ey Ja's stepmother finally began warming to her, they would work together on meal preparations. Ey Ja began sharing who the Lord is and what He had done in her life. One by one, beginning with her stepmother, the family members were won over to the truth as it was shared in love.

As UPCI missionaries in South Korea, my husband, William, our children, and I were present at the dedication of the church building that Ey Ja had built in Nam Hae. Toward the end of the powerful service, in the midst of a song about Jesus and His love, a young teenage girl fell to the floor and began writhing like a snake.

Recognizing a devil's outrage at the beautiful moving of the Holy Ghost, we gathered around the girl and began to rebuke the demonic spirit. Ey Ja restrained the girl as she hissed and tried to claw at us. The young pastor commanded the spirit to identify itself, and some of the people praying recognized the name it gave as the name of the girl's deceased grandmother. At the grandmother's death, this girl had developed serious health problems that doctors had been unable to figure out and treat.

At the last clinic the girl had visited, a nurse from the Nam Hae church had followed her and her mother out the door and told them the girl could be healed at our church. That is why the young teen was in the service that day. After she was delivered from demon possession, she calmed down, and, with a beautiful, smiling expression, began singing the previously interrupted song about Jesus along with the rest of the church. What a powerful church dedication it was!

5

South Asia

Bangladesh and Pakistan

Frances Day, Frances Foster

Bangladesh

Frances Day (2013-Active)

Frances Day began her missionary career in Bangladesh under the AIM program in 2013. After four years as an AIMer, she was appointed as an associate missionary, and advanced to intermediate missionary in 2019. Frances is TEFL/TESOL certified (teaching English as a foreign or second language). Before her missionary work, she was involved in community service and served in her home church in Thorp, Wisconsin. She also taught at Abundant Life Christian Academy in Thorp. Frances shares her personal testimony as she remains active in her missions work in Bangladesh. Here is her story:

> I was going through a horrible divorce when our two daughters, ages thirteen and ten, started going to church with a Pentecostal lady (who later became my best friend) and her daughters. My girls always invited me to attend church with them, but certain life experiences had taught me not to trust anything or anyone. One day my youngest daughter said, "Mom, I'm worried about Dad. If something happens to him, what will happen to his soul?" That really convicted my heart because I knew I wasn't right with God. So in August 1998 I went to church

with my daughters and their friends, repented, and received the gift of the Holy Ghost. Having been raised Baptist, I had been baptized using the titles Father, Son, and Holy Spirit. But after receiving the revelation of water baptism in Jesus' name, I was baptized in Jesus' name for the remission of my sins at age thirty-five. I always say I am a late bloomer, called into missions at the age of fifty. The good news is that eleventh-hour laborers receive the same pay as first-hour laborers. Thank you, Jesus! I'm so glad to be a child of the King!

I always dreamed of going to foreign lands. I prayed many prayers for Nigeria, but God never called me there. Instead, God sent Lionel Dabbs, a deputizing missionary from Singapore, to Wisconsin to meet me at the altar on a Sunday night and prophesy to me that God was calling me to the Asian nations. He sensed my reservation and said, "God would have me to tell you that a Chinese man will cross your path this week to confirm His word." The following Friday, I went to a convenience store by my house. When I came out and started across the parking lot, a Chinese man in Chinese-custom attire crossed in front of me. To this day I can't tell you if the Chinese man was a vision or if he was an angel sent from the Lord. All I know is that I began to weep. I asked the Lord to forgive me for doubting His call on my life for Asia and told Him I would go anywhere He sent me. He sent a Jamaican lady to the altar to tell me he was sending me out quickly.

In prayer, God told me He was going to give me a birthday gift. I told everyone. Many people thought I was crazy, but I knew I had heard God's voice. My birthday is February 26. On February 25 at 10:00 PM, my phone rang. The voice on the other end said, "Hello, Sister Day! This is Pastor James Corbin, superintendent and senior missionary to Bangladesh. Your name and contact information were given to me by Dr. Fred Childs. He said you would be a good assistant to my wife and me. I see you have an approved three-month AIM stay. Why not come here and see what God will say?" I said, "Okay, I will come."

God gave me a vision of a people I did not recognize. There was so much noise and chaos in the vision that I asked, "Lord, what is that noise? The sound is so loud." The Lord said, "It is drowning out My voice. I am sending you to this heathen nation to speak My name." My full budget was raised in one offering with some to spare. That budget lasted me for a year and a half, which extended my stay. Upon arriving in Bangladesh, Pastor Corbin drove me to my apartment. As we passed a mosque, I heard the "call to prayer" for the first time, and the vision came to life. I said, "Pastor, I am home." That was day one. It was March 21, 2013.

Every day as I walked to the church, I passed a pharmacy. The pharmacist and his wife would be sitting in front, so I would say, "Good morning" or "Good day" or "Good evening." At first they only nodded, but finally the husband asked, "What is your name? What are you doing in our country? Are you a preacher?" After telling him my name, I said, "No, I am not a preacher. I help the pastor in the church down the street." Three times the pharmacist asked if I was a preacher, and three times I answered no.

On my third day in Bangladesh, the pharmacist said, "Well, I run a home for men who are recovering drug addicts. I want you to come preach to them." I told him I would see what my pastor said. Pastor Corbin said, "Go! Preach!" At first I just talked to the men, saying, "You know, God doesn't want you to live like that." I held Bible studies with them and built upon what they had learned from the pharmacist, who was a good Roman Catholic doing all he knew to help them. Some of those former addicts were able to return to their families, some began to believe in Jesus, and some actually became Apostolic.

We helped host the 2015 AYC INDIA-FAITH in Calcutta, India. A sister brought her brother to the first night of the revival. He had been an alcoholic for forty-five years. His sister told him to come, and Jesus would set him free. He came in obedience to his elder sister. Skinny, frail-framed, and his body consumed by years of alcohol abuse, this man came to the altar. I asked him if he wanted to be delivered. He said, "Yes, I don't want to be a drunk." I said, "All you must do is repent, ask Jesus to forgive you, and turn from that sin. Jesus will come and forgive you and deliver you." He began to pray, saying, "Jesus, forgive me; I don't want to be a drunk anymore." Jesus delivered that man and filled him with the Holy Spirit. He and his sister danced and praised God with much joy! This was day one of the AYC revival services in India.

On day two of the revival service, the man who was delivered and filled with the Spirit the previous night returned and brought his friend with him. His friend had a problem; his seven-year-old daughter had just been sent home from the Apollo hospital with no hope of recovery. The mother and all the family were at the house around the little girl's bedside, waiting for her to take her final breath. But their friend who had been in bondage for forty-five years and was now delivered, healed, and filled with the Holy Ghost had one-day-old *great faith*. He told his friend that if he came to the revival service, the same Jesus that delivered him the previous night would do the same for his little girl.

This man's faith stirred my faith! Holy boldness rose in me, and at the appointed time I said, "Jesus is going to open a window of opportunity for us to pray for your daughter, and Jesus is going to raise her up off that death bed!" We began to worship with song and dance. I said, "Get your wife on the phone and have her place the phone by your daughter's ear." Then we prayed. Suddenly, we heard screaming on the other end of the phone. I said, "Ask your wife what is happening." She said, "Our daughter is sitting up and asking for food. She is walking around and hungry." Full strength had come back into her almost lifeless body. The girl's dad began crying and thanking Jesus, and Jesus filled him with the Holy Ghost. What faith!

One year later, ISIS attacked, and I had to flee from Bangladesh into India. I was invited to preach at a new house church, a dim-lit building a long way off the main path and down an alley. As we approached the house, a man greeted us. "Sister, do you remember me?" I said, "Please, friend, refresh my memory." He said, "A year ago you prayed for my little girl over the phone." "Oh, yes! I remember." This born-again man and his wife had opened their home to our local pastor to have church there. It was growing and had become a preaching point. That night I met his daughter and son and prayed with them.

During the 2018 Bangladesh Crusade, a blind lady was led by her daughter to the altar. The daughter stood her mother in front of me. She was wearing black sunglasses to disguise her blindness. I took her sunglasses off and saw the milky grey thickness that covered her eyes. I placed my hands over her eyes and prayed the prayer of faith, commanding blindness to leave her eyes in Jesus' name. I will never forget how the blindness melted crystal-clear tears in my hands. That lady began screaming, "I can see! I can see!" Her daughter snatched my hand and placed it on her head. She had a tumor that was pressing on her brain. Jesus dissolved that tumor. Oh, how we danced! Jesus had healed once again. I have seen the Lord do many miracles. We serve a mighty God!

In 2016, I was invited to a Southern Baptist Weekend Ladies Retreat. I didn't want to go, but felt I was supposed to go. My language teacher, who is also my friend, had invited me. She said, "Frances, you will make some good God-connections. Please come with me." I said okay and went with her. The theme of the retreat was "Refresh, Revive, Restore, and Refuel." The ladies who came from the US were medical missionaries, OB doctors, and OB nurses. They were sweet and kind as they ministered to the ladies by educating them on caring for their bodies. Devotions were refreshing because it was the Word of God. My friend was part of the administration and shared that I was also a missionary. The doctors and nurses were very kind to me when they heard my passion is to educate the women of Bangladesh to lead more productive lives. They gave me books and pamphlets in the Bangla language to teach the ladies of our churches.

Our capital church pastor's wife is an OB-surgical nurse. She now uses those materials to teach our ladies during family camp breakout sessions. I met so many wonderful ladies, some of whom are now Apostolic sisters. One Assembly of God pastor's wife befriended me and asked me to come to their city and host a ladies conference. She said, "They need the Holy Ghost." We went, and about one hundred ladies came and were taught the Word of God. Jesus filled forty-eight ladies with the Holy Ghost. One of those ladies was the A.G. pastor's daughter. We had been praying for a church in that city. The A.G. pastor's son was one of the graduates in the 2022 graduating class of the Guy E. Roam Bible College in Bangladesh. Baptized in Jesus' name and filled with the Holy Ghost, he is a great witness to his family and friends.

We have an unusual way of recruiting Bible school students. Our elders or pastors in villages see qualities in the young people in their villages that would make them excellent candidates for ministry. They make recommendations, and upon their recommendations, we accept the young people, and they come.

Our new Bible school students are usually either first-generation Apostolic or not Apostolic at all. The non-Apostolics are usually from Hindu or Muslim backgrounds with no Bible background. So, in the first few weeks, we take all the new students on a tour through the Bible, laying an Apostolic foundation. It gives all the students a foundational knowledge on who Jesus is, the new-birth experience, and what it means to be Apostolic. By the end of those few weeks, all the students are baptized in Jesus' name and filled with the Holy Ghost.

One young man named Samuel came to Bible school as a seventeen-year-old high school graduate who had no money for university. One of our elders came to him and said, "Samuel, I am going to take you to Dhaka to Bible college."

Samuel responded, "Me, Uncle? I'm Hindu. I don't know anything about Christianity." The elder said, "I don't care, Samuel. You're going, and God is going to use you mightily."

Now, Samuel was from the Santal tribe. They call Jesus "The Unknown God." So Samuel prayed to the Unknown God, saying, "Unknown God, if You are real and You really want me to go to this Christian college and learn about Christianity, then You need to send a friend with me—because if I go there and I come back, no one is going to be my friend." That night, Samuel asked his best friend if he wanted to go to the Christian college with him. His friend said yes!

Samuel asked, "Why?"

Samuel's friend said, "Last week, the pastor from that Christian college was here in our village teaching about water baptism in Jesus' name. He said if you repent of your sins and go down in the water in the name of Jesus, all your sins and sickness and diseases are buried in that water, and you come up out of the water clean, and it makes you a whole new man in Jesus' name." The friend continued, "Samuel, you know me. I am your best friend! Look at me. I used to have eczema all over my face and body. I took water baptism in Jesus' name, and now I am clean and made whole. So, yes, I want to go with you to that Christian college because I want to know what else that Jesus can do."

So the elder brought both of them with him. During the first few weeks of school, we laid a firm foundation of the name of God, the oneness of God, and the plan of salvation. For my morning class, I had my lesson prepared to teach how God called Samuel the prophet. That morning before class, there was a lot of conversation about the events that had occurred the night before. The new student, Samuel, began telling me what had happened during the night. He said he was sleeping in bed and heard someone call his name. He said he went to the elder's bedside and asked him if he had called him. The elder said, "No, I didn't call you. Go back to bed." He said it happened again, and this time the elder was very upset that his sleep was disturbed. He told Samuel to go back to bed and not wake him again. Samuel said he went back to bed but heard his name called a third time. So he went to the elder's bed, but this time, he saw the elder was sleeping and did not wake him. He went back to his bed to sleep. He thought it was a dream. As Samuel told me this, I began to cry. He said, "Sister, what is wrong?"

I told him and the class that this was our lesson for today—the life of Samuel the prophet and how God had called him. I shared the Bible story of Samuel and Eli. Then Samuel said, "Sister, I need to take water baptism in Jesus' name. I must take His name; He is calling me." I baptized Samuel in water in Jesus' name for the remission of his sins. When Samuel came up out of the water, Jesus filled him with the Holy Ghost. Samuel had the biggest smile on his face. You can always recognize Samuel for that beautiful smile. He is now in full-time ministry sharing the gospel of Jesus Christ.

I have had the privilege of baptizing hundreds of people in Jesus' name in Bangladesh. Sixty-five were Bible school students, and all of these former Bible school students are now in full-time ministry. I have also been privileged to see thousands filled with the Holy Ghost in Bangladesh. We are believing God for the refreshing and a one-million-soul revival! Witnessing what God has already done, it is easy to believe for a one-million-soul revival.

During the shelter-in-place quarantine of 2020, I continued my Bangla language study in the United States. Afterward, I completed deputation and returned to the field on June 26, 2021. I received a 2016 Toyota Noah minivan from Move the Mission, and I am so grateful! It makes life much easier to travel comfortably through the city.

The various responsibilities I have had so far include the following: preaching, Purpose Institute teacher, Bible college teacher, home Bible studies, ladies ministry, prayer coordinator, mentor, church planter (house churches), and anything else that needs my available hands. I have ministered in Dhaka (the capital city), Khulna, Dinajpur, Mymensingh, Rajshahi, Chattogram, Gazipur, and Satkhira.

This next term, if the Lord tarries and wills me to see it, I will be working with our pastors in the Mymensingh District five hours outside the capital city. I will go there monthly to rebuild the walls and establish a place for His name to be known and applied by salvation. Last week, I held a two-day Children's Church program where ten were baptized in Jesus' name and fifty-seven filled with the Holy Ghost. God is so good!

The mission field can sometimes get very lonely for a single lady, missing home, loved ones, friends, or maybe even your favorite unavailable snack. But I am never alone; God is my very best friend.

I advise future missionaries to take care of your health. I endured two major surgeries in Bangladesh. I know this didn't catch God by surprise, but it did me. Keep up with your prayer life. Stay rooted and grounded in Christ and in His Word. Stay submitted to your pastor and God's spiritual covering over your life. Keep effectual, fervent prayer warriors close. Be willing to be stretched. Keep a healthy balance in all things so you don't burn out. When you pour out, take time to refresh and refuel. Take naps, take tea breaks. Take the Word of God to the park or on your balcony. Take a walk in the middle of the day. Take a friend for coffee or lunch. Have a spa day. Listen to some music and relax. No guilt! No shame! These survival tools prepare you to pray, minister, teach, and preach. A healthy balance is essential.

What does the Lord require of you? "To do justly, to love mercy, and to walk humbly with your God" (Micah 6:8, NKJV). What should be your response? "Let the words of my mouth, and the meditation of my heart, be acceptable in thy sight, O LORD, my strength, and my redeemer" (Psalm 19:14).

I have hidden these verses in my heart as a reminder that the mouth speaks out of the abundance of the heart. I want to be a peace-speaker and doer of God's Word, in Jesus' name.

In the words of the old hymn, "Blessed Assurance,"

"This is my story, this is my song, praising my Savior all the day long."

Amen.

– Sister Frances Day

Pakistan

Frances Foster (Riddlesperger)

(1963–1975 / UPCI 1976–1981)

An American from Oregon, Frances Foster began her missionary work in Japan and India as a Trinitarian believer. Due to visa problems, Frances relocated to Pakistan in 1963. While there, she received a revelation of the oneness of God and baptism in Jesus' name.[1]

Frances returned to the United States and was baptized in Jesus' name in Burbank, California, by a UPC pastor, Bob Baglin.[2] She returned to Pakistan in 1968, becoming the "first missionary there to preach the oneness of God, baptism in the name of Jesus, and the infilling of the Holy Ghost with the initial evidence of speaking in tongues."[3]

Frances based out of Clarkabad in the Punjab province of east central Pakistan. She worked closely with a Pakistani minister, and they were able to register their church with the Pakistani government. "The gifts of the Spirit were in operation in nearly every service. They knew no rules about what they were 'supposed to do,' so they just let the Holy Ghost have His way. Some who only knew Punjabi were interpreting the messages in perfect Urdu. Prayer for the sick was a daily experience."[4]

At one point Frances wrote to the UPC secretary of Foreign Missions, asking that they send a missionary to Pakistan. By 1970, the Foreign Missions Board had appointed the first UPC missionaries to Pakistan, Everett and Lois Corcoran, and a couple of years later, Don and Saundra Hanscom.[5] Frances, too, would be appointed as a UPC missionary in 1976.

Frances hosted the Corcoran family of four upon their arrival, feeding them and setting up their beds with mosquito netting in the courtyard.[6] Her home was a two-room house of sunbaked bricks plastered with clay, cow dung, and straw. A tall wall surrounded the house's veranda and courtyard. To one side of the courtyard was the water pump, a tiny kitchen with a one-burner kerosene stove on the ground, another tiny "shower room" with a dipper and pail of tepid water, and a curtained latrine—a hole dug in the earth. The courtyard floor was plastered with cow dung, which made a hard surface when dry but a slippery surface during the rainy season.[7]

Frances had chickens and one layer hen for eggs (a luxury), and their roaming area was also in the courtyard, where they kept down the bug population. The house and courtyard walls frequently sported harmless lizards, which also helped curb the mosquito and bug populations. Bats, which hung from the ceiling joists sleeping during the day, would awaken at dusk and sweep through the house and outside to feast on bugs at night.[8]

Clarkabad had been a British village during British rule and therefore had electricity, albeit sporadically.[9] By this time in 1971, Pakistan had sixty million people and was 97 percent Muslim.[10] The Pakistani women had a strict dress code, and Frances dressed accordingly. The appropriate local dress for women in Punjab consisted of voluminous leggings wrapped over in the front, a long, knee-length tunic over the leggings, and a long headscarf, always worn when men were present.[11]

Frances traveled with the other missionaries to the Urdu language school in the mountain town of Murree in the Himalayan foothills. She took morning classes, watched the children during their parents' afternoon class sessions, and helped with the marketing.[12]

Frances invited the sixteen preachers with whom she worked to meet the Corcorans, and they all joined the UPC. When Asia Regional Director Harry Scism visited and observed Frances's work, he encouraged her to apply for appointment as a UPC missionary, which she did.[13] After fleeing Pakistan in 1971 due to the imminent war between East and West Pakistan, Frances returned in 1973 under UPC endorsement as she awaited her UPC missionary appointment in 1976.[14]

Through the years, many children in Pakistan had been baptized in Jesus' name, had received the Holy Ghost, and had become prayer warriors and evangelists to their own families.[15] In 1973, Frances began teaching Sunday school seminars to train village church women. Later, she taught prayer and child evangelism at pastors' seminars. She helped set up Sunday schools in village churches and taught the church and neighborhood children during the hour before services. Later, some of the Bible school students became excellent Sunday school teachers. Frances arranged a lending library of visual aids, one month at a time, for the pastors to pick up and return when they came monthly to the headquarters with their church and Sunday school reports.[16]

In 1981, Frances retired from missionary work and took her final flight back to the United States as a single missionary. During her many years of ministry in Pakistan, she saw multitudes healed, delivered, baptized in Jesus' name, and filled with the Holy Ghost. She saw the Lord's hand leading herself and others as He directed their efforts for His kingdom.[17]

At age seventy, nine years after she departed from Pakistan, and after asking the Lord if she was always to be alone, the Lord provided Frances with a husband—a seventy-eight-year-old widower and long-time Apostolic minister. They resided in California. Within three months of their wedding, the Lord provided a way for Frances Riddlesperger and her husband, Clarence, to travel to Pakistan for three weeks of preaching and teaching in her beloved churches and the Bible school. Upon their arrival in Clarkabad, where Frances had long ministered, the thriving church had them clothed in the traditional bride and groom garments of Pakistan and gave them a lovely, flower-strewn reception.[18]

Even in their final years, Frances and Clarence Riddlesperger made a powerful team for the Lord. Frances Foster Riddlesperger, born on October 11, 1920, passed to her eternal reward on October 2, 2002. Clarence lived until 2008.

6

Southeast Asia and Oceania

Thailand, Java, Tonga

Elly Hansen, Edith Berthoux, Crystal Reece

Thailand

Elly Hansen (1952 arrival in Thailand / 1974 appointment by UPCI–1987)

God so loved the world that He called messengers from North America and Europe to communicate His love to the people of Thailand. Readers of UPCI missionary news in the 1960s will recall stories about the calling of William ("Billy") and Shirley Cole to Thailand and their remarkable missionary ministry. Fewer readers will have read about a single lady missionary whose arrival in Thailand from Denmark predated the arrival of the Coles.

Elly Hansen, a native of Denmark, was a missionary nurse in northern Thailand for seventeen years before she heard the Apostolic message and embraced it. In 1974, Elly received her appointment as a United Pentecostal Church missionary. A *1984 Foreign Missions Story* reported that Elly was busily engaged in many aspects of the work: pastoring a church, teaching in a Bible school, holding seminars, translating the International Bible Course into Thai, and printing it. In between duties, she visited churches throughout Thailand and helped with youth work and camps. Elly parented many children through her orphanage, and many of her "children" were saved due to her influence.[1]

Interestingly, Elly Hansen arrived in Thailand fifteen years before Billy Cole's evangelistic ministry birthed the Oneness Pentecostal church in the country. After the Coles' five-year term of service in Thailand, they successfully nationalized the UPC there. By 1972, about ten thousand people regularly attended UPC churches in Thailand, with at least five thousand baptized and filled with the Holy Ghost. The nationalized church had seventeen national leaders and ninety-five churches with Thai ministers (*1972 Foreign Missions Status Report*). Although Buddhism dominated the lives of 90 percent of the Thai people, thousands converted to Apostolic truth upon hearing about God's love.[2]

In 1952, two decades before the Coles nationalized the United Pentecostal Church in Thailand, red-headed Elly arrived in Thailand with a firm resolve to share God's love. Elly's eventual connection with the Coles demonstrates how God miraculously orchestrates His plan to reveal the truth. Elly's fascinating story, as told in the book *Following Jesus All the Way: Elly*, by Elly Hansen and Mary Wallace, merits a place in UPCI missionary history. Some selected highlights from this book as well as *Apostolic Pioneers in Missions* reveal the uniqueness of how God sent missionaries from two continents to deliver His Word to a country immersed in false religion. Also, the story shows how a God-called, Spirit-filled lady received a revelation of God's oneness after arriving in Thailand as an appointed missionary of another organization.

Elly's homelife did not prepare her for Christian ministry. Her father was "totally anti-God and antichurch." He employed young Elly as a bartender and dancer. Her lifestyle unexpectedly changed when she accepted an invitation to church and heard the gospel. She decided, "I will follow Jesus."

Her firm decision angered her father. He declared, "Well, follow Jesus then! See where He will lead you. You have had your last meal here." As a seventeen-year-old, Elly packed her bag and left their family-operated hotel that day, never again to tend the bar and dance to delight the hotel guests. Thirteen years passed before she again entered her family home.[3]

Elly walked the streets wondering where to go, but she felt assured that God was with her. She prayed, "God, I don't know what to do. Will You help me?"

As she walked, a voice interrupted her thoughts: "Where are you going?"

She looked up to see the face of a lady who had once taken her to Sunday school as a small child. When Elly shared her story, the kind Baptist lady offered her a place in her home. Elly found a job in a difficult job market and became active in the church where she had decided to follow Jesus earlier.[4]

As Elly faithfully attended and worked in the church, she began to sense a call to greater things. In prayer, she saw a copper-red road winding through a dark green jungle. At the end of the road, she saw a cross on top of a church. Then she heard a voice say, "I want you to be used by God."[5]

Desiring to be used by God, Elly became active in the Evangelical church and diligently studied God's Word. In contemplating missionary work, she learned she would need training as a teacher or nurse in order to receive a missionary appointment. She decided on nursing[6] and began training at a psychiatric hospital in Birkerød, about twenty kilometers from Copenhagen. She worked dayshift and took university classes at night.[7]

War clouds gathered over Europe as Elly pursued her studies. Adolf Hitler's rise to power and the German rearmament threatened Denmark. In May 1939, Denmark signed a nonaggression pact with Germany and repeatedly assured Germany of its neutrality. Despite this pact, Germany secretly planned and executed Operation Weserübung, the invasion of Denmark and Norway.

On April 9, 1940, Nazi soldiers poured into Copenhagen, took over businesses and newspapers, and confiscated vehicles and other equipment. German troops came ashore from Danish ports, and bombers flew over defenseless cities. The German minister handed the Danish government a memorandum demanding submission. The Danes initially submitted to the occupation, reasoning that compliance would protect the country from war disasters. However, the Danish ambassador to the United States thought differently and requested the American government's endorsement. British troops and the US Air Force provided resources from bases in the Faroe Islands and Greenland, both then under the control of Denmark. A handful of Greenland Danes patrolled Greenland's east coast, the world's largest island. During the occupation, the greater part of the Danish merchant fleet (about two hundred ships) sailed worldwide out of German reach.[8]

One late evening, as Elly hurried back to the Birkerød Hospital, a young man fell in step beside her, explaining that he lived near the hospital. He shared that he knew her father, Christian Hansen, and that his father owned the bus company. After boarding the bus, the two continued talking. He requested permission to come by the hospital to see Elly. As it turned out, their friendship blossomed into romance. Soon after her twenty-first birthday in July 1942, he surprised her with an engagement ring. She accepted his proposal.[9]

After her engagement, Elly returned to her home church for a prayer meeting. As she prayed, God reminded her of her missionary calling and that her friend was not a Christian. Elly's friends prayed with her for three months until Elly finally acknowledged that she would be stepping out of God's will in marrying a non-Christian. She decided to follow Jesus. The next time her fiancé visited, she humbly acknowledged, "I have made a wrong step. You must forget about me."[10] Although her decision displeased her father, and although her former fiancé later tried to renew the friendship after Elly had begun her missionary work and returned from Thailand for a visit, she remained firm in her commitment to follow Jesus.[11]

After three years in Birkerød, Elly returned to her hometown to begin medical training in a hospital, where she and a group of courageous nurses formed an underground resistance group to provide an escape route for Jews. The nurses bitterly resented the brutality of the Germans. Elly had seen Nazis grab elderly Jewish women by their hair and drag them down stairwells. She knew that Nazis occupied Jewish homes after throwing their furniture out the windows and burning it. The nurses developed a scheme for instructing the Jews to take the train to a poorly guarded station where they would be picked up and taken to a safe place. One hindrance was the curfew. Elly offered a solution: "I work here in this hospital. I am allowed out after curfew. I can ride my bicycle to Holti (the train station), walk these people through the woods, get them into a car early in the morning, and drive them to that church [safe place] we have been told about." The nurses gave the Jews the code name "lemons." They would send messages to helpers, such as, "Could you pick up a dozen lemons tonight at ten o'clock?" Some churches offered hiding places for the Jews. One pastor hid as many as 250 Jews in the basement of his church.[12]

Getting the Jews from the safe places to fishing boats for passage to Sweden was a problem, but the nurses found ways to entertain and distract the German soldiers while Jews boarded the fishing boats. Having worked as a barmaid for years, Elly knew how to talk to lonely soldiers. The nurses' efforts helped the underground operation save about seven thousand Danish and German Jews.

At one point Elly was warned, "If the Nazis find out you have that gun, you may get shot."[13]

Elly responded, "Better to be shot than sent to one of those awful death camps in Germany."[14] She expressed trust in God but also said God helps those who help themselves. She carried a knife and pepper spray in her pockets for protection. Ultimately, God protected Elly as she pursued her nurse's training and aided the resistance during the war years. When the war ended in May 1945, Elly joined her fellow countrymen as they rejoiced in the streets.[15]

Though the war prolonged Elly's training as a nurse, she never lost her desire to be a missionary. She completed her nurse's training in 1949 when she was in her late twenties. However, she still needed Bible-school training in order to be appointed by the Danish Mission Forbund, a Danish missionary society associated with the Hudson Taylor China Inland Mission. She chose to attend London Bible College. After six years of medical training and work in the underground during World War II, she looked forward to Bible studies. During her nurse's training, she had worked to pay her education costs. She went to Bible college, believing God to meet her needs. He did not fail her!

The faith that had filled Elly's heart at age seventeen when she chose to follow the Lord continued to sustain her. The college taught students never to request money but to trust God.[16]

Though Elly had learned English in her earlier school years, she feared that her English would not be good enough for Bible college since several people in London had commented, "We can't understand you." But three months later she passed the English language courses and was sent out to speak at gospel meetings.[17]

During her training Elly had felt she was called to China; however, the door to China slammed firmly shut at the end of her first year of study. After speaking at a small-town church, she went into the countryside and climbed a hill carrying her Bible to talk to God. She asked God, "I thought I was called to China. Now what am I to do? Where do You want me to go? I need some answers." After a time of prayer, she heard a whisper in her heart: "I want you to go to Siam" (Thailand). As a ship sailed northeast, carrying Elly's letter to the mission board back in Denmark, another ship sailed west, carrying a message to Elly expressing a need for a missionary in Thailand. Elly continued her studies while developing plans to go to Thailand with the Worldwide Evangelistic Crusade from the United States. As it turned out, she spent her first two years in Thailand under their leadership.[18]

After completing her Bible college training, Elly returned to Denmark to work in her old hospital to raise money for her ticket to Thailand. One night when she came on duty, a young, deathly ill girl from her church was admitted to the hospital. Dr. Enger Krog told Elly, "We don't have anything to help this girl."

Elly declared, "We must pray. I believe in prayer."

"You do?" cried the doctor as her eyes lit up.

"I do! Let's pray." Elly laid her hands on the child, and the Lord healed her.

Dr. Krog took the girl into the ward and told eight women, "God has performed a miracle!" Four of the women turned to God, and Elly became a close friend of the lady doctor. Elly's faith grew as she witnessed God's miraculous power.

In December 1951, Dr. Krog asked Elly, "Have you been baptized in the Holy Ghost?"

Elly responded, "I must have the Holy Ghost, or I wouldn't be able to get a true understanding of the Bible. So I suppose I have."[19]

Still, Dr. Krog's question caused Elly to pray and search the Scriptures, since she had not spoken in tongues. On May 12, 1952, she received the Holy Ghost, and later that year she sailed for Thailand to begin her missionary work.[20] For many years, beginning in late 1952, she cared for leprosy patients in northern Thailand amid poverty and primitive living conditions. After serving as a midwife for a leprous couple, the parents disappeared, leaving baby Tonghey in Elly's care. Tonghey became the first of forty-six children that Elly helped raise, some of whom she adopted.[21]

In August 1959, Elly recognized that she needed to consult a doctor due to weight loss, fatigue, and coughing up blood. Test results showed that she had tuberculosis. The Danish doctor in Bangkok ordered that she return to Copenhagen for treatment. When she went to the Danish embassy to ensure she could obtain a visa to return to

Thailand, the agent "sent her in a car to take care of her affairs and radioed via East Asiatic ships to her missions board back in Denmark, 'Put her in the Royal Hospital in Copenhagen. They have a TB ward there.'"[22]

Before leaving Thailand, Elly sought out her Presbyterian minister friend, Boon Mak, requesting prayer for healing. He and two other pastors anointed her and prayed earnestly. She reported, "A stream of something went through my body."[23]

When Elly arrived at the hospital in Denmark, Chief of Staff Dr. Wuarberg (one of the top ten men in Danish medicine) attended her. It just so happened that Elly had helped hide Dr. Wuarberg from the Germans during the war. He ordered a complete set of X-rays for her—forty-eight pictures—plus other tests. As Elly awoke from anesthesia, he asked her, "What kind of doctor did you see in Bangkok? Perhaps he has sent the wrong X-rays." Elly assured him that those were her X-rays.[24]

After ten days of reviewing her case, the doctor asked, "What has happened to you? You couldn't possibly be healed just because you flew from Bangkok to Copenhagen."[25]

Elly explained, "Well, Dr. Wuarberg, between those two sets of X-rays, I had three evangelical pastors in Bangkok anoint me with oil and pray for me in the name of the Lord Jesus Christ. . . . If I am what you say I am, then God has healed me."[26]

Though the good Jewish doctor did not like the name of Jesus Christ, he agreed that "Jehovah God does still work miracles as He did in the time of Moses."[27]

Elly remained in the hospital under the doctor's care as she regained her strength. He ordered food and care to rebuild her body to normal size so she could return to

Thailand. During her hospital stay, he invited her to teach and preach to all the university medical students, telling them about her work in Thailand. As she shared about her work and answered questions, she testified about becoming a Christian. During her stay in the hospital, her Presbyterian minister friend, Boon Mak, stopped to visit her while en route to America to visit a friend. In July 1960, after Boon Mak's visit, Elly flew back to Bangkok.[28]

Elly continued her missionary work caring for about nineteen hundred leprosy patients (which had resulted in her tuberculosis diagnosis), unaware that God was designing more significant plans for her. Her work was associated with the Presbyterian church pastored by Boon Mak. As it happened, Boon Mak was unable to locate his friend in America. Instead, he met Billy Cole, a UPC pastor in West Virginia, who taught him Apostolic truth and baptized him in Jesus' name. Boon Mak returned to Thailand with an understanding of the oneness of God. He began baptizing Thai people in Jesus' name, including the man who would later become the superintendent of the UPC of Thailand. When Elly heard this new doctrine at Boon Mak's church, she considered it heresy.

Despite rejecting the Oneness doctrine, Elly attended conferences at Boon Mak's church and ultimately met Billy Cole. For three years she prayed and studied a book Billy gave her on the oneness of God. In April 1965, Frank Munsey baptized her in Jesus' name.[29] Unfortunately, her missionary board heard about her acceptance of Jesus Name baptism and withdrew her support. Once again she was homeless at the age of forty-one. She fasted and prayed for three days, packed up her belongings, and moved to the marketplace to live humbly among the Thai people. She soon started a Saturday Bible school and then a Sunday morning service. God provided for her needs and blessed her ministry with miracle after miracle.[30]

In 1970, five years after her missions board removed her support, Elly dedicated a two-story, forty-by-sixty-foot teakwood building in Phran Kratai. She held church services on the first floor and lived comfortably on the second floor. Despite being left homeless and destitute on two occasions, she obeyed God's Word and touched countless lives with love and truth. God indeed used Elly as she nursed lepers in the jungle areas and later built and pastored an Apostolic church.[31]

In 1974, with encouragement from friends, Elly applied for and received an appointment as a United Pentecostal Church International missionary. She faithfully served as a UPCI missionary for over twelve years until her death from cancer on October 11, 1987. She had devoted thirty-five years as a God-called missionary to the Thai people. At her request, she was buried in a small Christian cemetery in Thailand near where she had labored for over three decades.[32]

Java

Edith Berthoux (1947–1952 or later)

Edith's name appears on the 1947 list of early UPC missionaries to Java, which indicates she had received appointment. In addition, her name appears on the 1948 missionary list as "on the field."[33] She served in Java alongside George and Helen White. A post in *The Evolving World of Foreign Missions* states that W. R. and Sallie Pardue were appointed to assist the Whites and Edith Berthoux in Java in 1950.[34] The only other mention of Edith in *The Evolving World of Foreign Missions* states that she was recommended for appointment to Java in 1952.[35] This reflects the earlier policy that missionaries met the Foreign Missions Board for reappointment after serving on the field. Unfortunately, no other information about Edith's work in Java was found to verify how long she served on the field.

Tonga

Crystal Reece (1996–2017)

When contacted about her missionary work as a single woman, Crystal compiled a summary of her two decades in UPCI missions.[36] She became the extra hands and feet needed by missionaries already serving on the field. Her work also involved a season of laboring alone on a remote island. Crystal's book, *Island Splashes*,[37] provides additional details about her time there.

Crystal began her missionary ministry in Vanuatu as an AIMer working with Lee and Becky Sherry. Appointed in 1996, she served in Vanuatu from April 1998 to June 1999. Her primary duties were Bible school teaching and assisting the Sherrys. She became the music director for the English service at All Nations Church. She also taught at the youth camp.

After her time in Vanuatu, Crystal served in the Kingdom of Tonga with Bennie and Pat Blunt from May 2001 to November 2006. In Tonga, she filled the roles of Bible school coordinator and teacher. She also assisted the Blunts and ministered in the local churches. In addition, she helped with the youth and Sunday school camps and ladies programs. She became a licensed minister with the UPCI during her time in Tonga.

In January 2010, Crystal was appointed as a UPCI intermediate missionary. Before her deputation from February 2011 through May 2011, she served again in Vanuatu assisting Lee and Becky Sherry. She ministered on the outer island of Espiritu Santos. She taught English, Basic Skills, and Study Habits at the Preparatory School, filling in for a missionary on leave. She also spoke in local churches for pastors who had been her former students. On returning to the States for deputation, she ministered in forty-five states and six Canadian provinces between July 2011 and September 2013.

On her return to the Kingdom of Tonga, Crystal served in various roles from December 2013 to December 2017. She served as the administrator of the Bible school and the principal teacher. She was the sole missionary living on the island for over three years, with the closest missionary over five hundred miles away. She became immersed in the Tongan culture and built friendships among the Tongans, Australians, and New Zealanders. The only Americans were short-term Peace Corps workers.

Crystal pastored a local congregation in the village of Nuku Nuku. As the head of the Bible school, she served on the General Board. She preached in local churches, camps, ladies conferences, and general conferences. She taught Bible studies and officiated at baptisms, weddings, and funerals. She organized, developed, and executed many programs throughout the islands. Her involvement included painting, cleaning, mowing grass, and mending fences to provide upkeep for the headquarters building and village church.

In sharing a summary of her missionary work, Crystal expressed that she still desires to be involved in global missions and prays that it will happen. Crystal wrote,

"Missions is my life, and my heart is to follow my beloved Jesus everywhere He sends me." She shared that the motto of Tonga is "ko Otua mo Tonga Ko hoko tofi," which means "my God and Tonga are my inheritance." Tonga's motto had literally become the motto of her life.

At the time of this writing, she is serving in North American Missions as a pastor in a rural area in Tennessee.

PART II
AFRICA

7

Liberia, West Africa

Pearl Graham (Holmes), Georgia Regenhardt, Gladys Robinson, Pauline Gruse, Geneva Bailey, Valda Russell, Laverne Collins Else Lund, Ena Hylton

In the early 1820s, freed American slaves began a settlement in the country we know today as Liberia. The country would go on to become Africa's first independent republic in 1847. With English as a common language and a government modeled after that of the United States, it is understandable why it became the first African country to attract North American missionaries. Liberia's open door for establishing mission compounds with schools for Liberian children drew the interest of North American Pentecostals, who felt a call to obey the Great Commission.

Single women missionaries met the distinctive need for teachers on these mission stations. As their biographies show, these women were pioneers and visionaries in establishing new mission compounds and reaching remote areas with the gospel. As a result, single women have significantly contributed to the UPCI's missionary work in Liberia, West Africa.

More single ladies have been appointed to Liberia by the UPCI than any other country. When the United Pentecostal Church was formed in 1945, several Pentecostal missionaries in Liberia became UPC-appointed missionaries. At least four couples transitioned to the UPC from their appointments with the PCI and PAW. Among the couples were Aaron and Pearl Holmes. Interestingly, Pearl had previously served in Liberia as a single lady (Pearl Graham) before a UPC presence was established there. Her story is included here because of the impact of her mission in Liberia.

In 1946, the UPC appointed Georgia Regenhardt, its first single woman missionary to Liberia who had not served under another Oneness organization. Since 1945, the UPCI has appointed twenty-two missionary units (counting a couple as one unit) to Liberia. Eight of these appointees have been single women. This chapter includes Pearl Graham's story in Liberia as a single woman missionary before the merger of 1945 as well as the biographical highlights of the eight UPCI-appointed single women who served in Liberia between 1946 and 1975.

Readers of *SENT! Volume 3, Africa,* by Darline Royer may recognize a similarity with some of the following accounts as some of that material is used here.

Pearl Graham (Holmes) (1896 arrival in Liberia through 1916 as single / 1945–1961)

Pearl's story stands as a hallmark of Liberia's mission story. She was born in Little Rock, Arkansas, and attended Arkansas Baptist College. As a student, she developed a concern for the people of Africa, whom she called "my people." She wrote, "God, who works in mysterious ways, touched my mother's heart to give her two daughters a trip to Africa."[1]

Pearl arrived in Liberia ten years before the Azusa Street outpouring of the Holy Ghost, and fifty years before the formation of the United Pentecostal Church. As an adventuress with her mother and sister, she traveled by boat to Liberia in 1896. Though not a Pentecostal by experience, she began feeling a burden for the Liberian people while still aboard the ship. What was intended as a pleasure trip turned into a lifetime mission for Pearl. She ministered in Liberia for sixty-three years and became known among Oneness Pentecostals as Mother Holmes.

In 1916, twenty years after she arrived in Liberia, Pearl married widower Aaron Holmes, who had been living in Liberia for two years. At the time, Pearl was working with a Baptist mission. According to Pearl's letter published in the *Pentecostal Herald* (April 1950), Pearl, her mother, and her sister received the baptism of the Holy Ghost in 1924 as they obeyed Acts 2:38. That same year the Holmeses moved to an interior area and established the Zoradee Mission, which still exists. She expressed happiness about teaching others and seeing them filled with the Holy Spirit, speaking in other tongues. Zoradee became the site of the first outpouring of the Holy Ghost in Liberia. Pearl worked in Liberia for forty-three years before making a trip back to the States.

Though Pearl married, she spent nearly twenty years as a single missionary. More of Pearl and Aaron's story (1945–1961) can be read in *SENT! Volume 3, Africa*. Before their UPC affiliation, the Holmeses had been supported by the PAW and PCI.

Pearl's husband, Aaron, suffered a fatal heart attack in 1958 at age seventy-three as he was traveling in the US to raise funds. Sadly, Pearl was unable to attend her husband's funeral due to a broken leg from a fall.[2] However, friends later paid her way to America. While there, she attended a missionary meeting in Connecticut where missionaries and elders gathered around her and prayed. As they prayed, her crippled leg began shaking. Someone asked, "Mother Holmes, what is the matter?"

She responded, "What is the matter? God has healed my leg! Glory to His name!" She left the meeting without her cane.[3]

After sixty-five years in Liberia, Pearl Holmes retired in 1961 and returned to the US. She passed away on January 1, 1964. She and her husband, Aaron, were posthumously inducted into the UPCI Order of the Faith at the 2021 General Conference.

While serving in Liberia in 1946, Pearl introduced a newly appointed missionary lady to Liberia—Georgia Regenhardt from Mississippi. The following year, another single lady, Gladys Robinson, joined Georgia Regenhardt. Six other single women served in Liberia as UPC missionaries: Pauline Gruse, Valda Russell, Else Lund, Ena Hylton, Laverne Collins, and Jean Bailey. Their labors blended with other missionary couples in the twentieth century to plant the Apostolic message and nurture a growing, vibrant church. May their stories foster faith and vision for global missions in this twenty-first century.

Georgia Regenhardt (1946–1960)

Appointed on March 27, 1946, Georgia Regenhardt made her maiden trip to Liberia in the company of Missionary Pearl Graham Holmes. Their flight encountered delays, difficulties, and an airplane without heat, making them wish for fur-lined parkas. Georgia was thankful to be in the company of an experienced missionary. Upon arrival at the airport on December 28, 1946, Georgia and Pearl rode a bus forty miles to Monrovia, Liberia's capital. For three days, Pearl provided accommodations for Georgia at a house she rented in the city and where her daughter operated a business. From there, they went their separate ways—Pearl returning to Zoradee Mission and Georgia heading to Maheh Mission to replace Missionaries Louis and Helen Haney as they furloughed.

Georgia's call to missions came when she received the Holy Ghost as a widowed mother with three children, ages ten, seven, and five. In May 1917, at age fifteen, she had married Henry Regenhardt. They had realized their need for God's help and joined the Missionary Baptist Church. Tragically, Henry had died in 1928 after a five-day illness, leaving Georgia alone at age thirty-one to raise their three children. After her husband's death, Georgia moved from Tennessee to Corinth, Mississippi, where she became a factory worker.

In Corinth, she attended a Pentecostal tent meeting conducted by Pastor A. D. Gurley, and was baptized in the name of Jesus. In a cottage prayer meeting, she received the Holy Ghost. As she spoke in tongues, she had a vision of dark faces pleading with outstretched hands. She whispered to herself, "I am called to Africa!"

After her conversion, Georgia became active in church ministry. She taught Sunday school, promoted missions, and did whatever her pastor requested. She read and studied her Bible, rising an hour or two earlier than necessary each day to pray and study before going to work. In 1945, when the Pentecostal Bible Institute opened in Tupelo, Mississippi, Georgia enrolled and also served as a dorm mother. Her daughters had married by this time, and her eighteen-year-old son was self-sufficient. She felt it was time to pursue her call to Africa. She applied, and the UPC Foreign Missions Board granted her an appointment on March 27, 1946.

As recorded by Nona Freeman, Georgia had made a prayerful commitment when she received the Holy Ghost and sensed God's call to Africa. She had prayed, "O Lord, however long the road may be, help me prepare myself to go when the time comes."[4] More than a decade later, Georgia stepped onto African soil. She had received the Spirit at age thirty-three and arrived in Africa at age forty-four.

Georgia's missionary life began after her bus trip from the airport to Monrovia and three days in the city with Mother Holmes. On December 30, she rode a motor launch for three hours and then walked another hour to a Lutheran mission. From there, she began the twelve-hour trek through Liberia's "bush" to Maheh Mission, her place of assignment. Missionary Haney, whom she would replace, had arranged for four men to carry Georgia through the jungle in a hammock; however, she walked for short intervals to give the carriers a rest. When the dense blackness of the jungle and treacherous river crossings brought fear, the Lord's Word spoke peace to her heart: "The eternal God is thy refuge, and underneath are the everlasting arms" (Deuteronomy 33:27).

Louis and Helen Haney gave Georgia a royal welcome to Maheh Mission, a compound with fourteen buildings, nice lawns, level paths, extensive orchards, and vegetable gardens. They introduced her to twenty-five children at Maheh. She would be responsible for their housing, feeding, schooling, discipline, and spiritual training. The children won her heart, but she felt overwhelmed by the sense of responsibility.

On January 6, 1947, Helen Haney escorted Georgia to Beajah Mission, a two-hour walk, where she met Missionaries Otis and Rozelle Petty and Pauline Gruse.

As it turned out, a few months later Georgia assumed the load of the Beajah Mission along with Maheh. Due to the failing health of the Pettys, Missions Director Wynn Stairs ordered the close of the Beajah Mission, with everything to be turned over to the Maheh Mission.

The Pettys asked Georgia to take over the care of the Beajah Mission children. Though feeling incapable, she prayed and found the courage to say, "I'll do my best."

The Pettys offered to stay until May to help with the transfers and adjustments. They had been informed that a new missionary named Gladys Robinson would arrive by May to assist with the load.

On March 16, 1947, the mission held a farewell service for the Haneys, and they departed for Monrovia the following day. Georgia wrote a letter dated March 21 with this opening: "Here I am, a lone missionary in the wilds of Africa—so busy I can hardly eat or sleep. I not only have the work the Haneys did but am cleaning up and making room for the Pettys, with continual interruptions. My mind is so busy, it doesn't allow me to sleep much." Besides the addition of the children from Beajah Mission, other needy children were brought to the mission as well.

Before May ended, Georgia declared Africa to be a wonderful place for developing patience: she had contracted a bad case of poison ivy, Gladys's arrival was delayed, the baby kept her up at night, her refrigerator didn't arrive, and few letters came. Due to sickness, the Pettys had to leave sooner than planned. Above all, Georgia longed for revival. On a positive note, Pearl Holmes maintained her friendship with Georgia, which was a mutual blessing and encouragement. In late June, Pearl wrote to Georgia, offering to stay in Monrovia to await Gladys Robinson's arrival and help her get to Maheh.

Finally, in August 1947, Gladys Robinson arrived at Maheh to work with Georgia. They shared the responsibilities of the mission school and church and began evangelizing the surrounding villages. They trekked through the bush for two, three, or more days accompanied by students to help carry food, bedding, clothes, lanterns, and boiled water. Their sacrifices brought rejoicing as Liberians responded to the Apostolic message. The Maheh Mission also experienced revival as students and their parents were baptized and filled with the Spirit.

In May 1948, Georgia found herself alone once again at Maheh when Gladys left to open a mission at Bomi Hills, the location of an iron ore mine within a two- to three-hour walk from Maheh. Before she left, however, Gladys graciously took care of the Maheh Mission while Georgia spent a restful week in Monrovia. On her return to Maheh, Georgia awaited word about the arrival of Missionary Pauline Gruse, who would oversee the mission when Georgia furloughed the following year. As it turned out, Pauline arrived just after Christmas.

The three missionary ladies experienced many things during 1949. They were excited when Gladys arrived with a new pickup for the use of both missions. With the newly constructed road to Bomi Hills, the missionaries could drive to Monrovia. Sadly, two of their promising students returned to their superstitious customs the same week the pickup arrived. On a good note, Georgia completed building a new mud-walled church on the mission. With transportation, the ladies began reaching more towns with the gospel.

As 1949 ended, Pauline took over the operation of Maheh Mission as Georgia made plans to leave for deputation. Georgia arrived stateside in time for the best

Christmas ever with her family. Pastor A. D. Gurley welcomed Georgia to a homecoming service on January 8, 1950, in Corinth, Mississippi. Some days later, she enrolled again at Pentecostal Bible Institute to complete her training. After graduating in 1951, she boarded a ship in New Orleans on May 16 and arrived back in Monrovia on June 6.

Refreshed, Georgia returned to her work at Maheh with vigor. Gladys Robinson had gone on furlough, and the Pettys were serving at Bomi Hills. New missionaries came—Hubert and Dorothy Parks followed by Geneva Bailey. Gladys returned from furlough, but had to leave three months later due to cancer. Notice of her death reached Georgia in December 1953. Georgia found solace in persistent attention to her duties. All too soon, another term ended, and a third deputation began.

In the spring of 1956, Georgia returned to Maheh. A mission car of her own and better roads made her third term easier. Valda Russell, appointed in 1953, became another of her missionary coworkers. After completing a third term in Liberia, Georgia returned to the US in 1960 and joined the staff at Pentecostal Bible Institute as a teacher and dean of women. She continued in these roles until 1970, and served as librarian for PBI until 1972. Georgia entered the hospital on July 21, 1976, and passed away six hours later.

Memories of Georgia remain with me today. As a ten-year-old child, I met Georgia when she studied at Pentecostal Bible Institute before she left for Liberia. My childhood acquaintance with Georgia imprinted missions in my mind. As I record the stories of these single missionary ladies, I pray that many young women of the twenty-first century will heed God's call.

The following sources provided information about Georgia's story and other stories that follow:

- *Apostolic Pioneers in Missions* by Dorsey Burk (UPCI, 2012)
- *Profiles of Pentecostal Missionaries*, compiled by Mary Wallace (Word Aflame Press, 1986)
- *The Evolving World of Foreign Missions* by Daniel L. Scott Sr.

Gladys Robinson (1946–1953)

Gladys's study at Apostolic Bible College in Tulsa, Oklahoma, equipped her for missionary teaching. She sensed a vindication of her call to missions when she heard Missionary Peter Jensen prophesy at a meeting in Carterville, Illinois, that someone in the audience had a call to Africa. The missionary board endorsed her in 1946. She arrived in Liberia on July 31, 1947. Her assignment to the Beajah Mission with Otis and Roselle Petty changed to the Maheh Mission with Georgia Regenhardt when the Beajah Mission closed due to the Pettys' failing health and insufficient funds.

Gladys envisioned and founded the Bomi Hills Mission. When she heard in 1948 that the US Steel Corporation of America planned to construct an iron ore mining camp at Bomi Hills, she visualized plans for a school and church at this location. She appealed to Missions Director Wynn Stairs for funding. Deeply impressed, he sponsored Bomi Hills until missionary funding became available to operate another mission station. Gladys joined the team working to clear the jungle, making space for school rooms, a church, and her humble home. Along with managing the mission station, Gladys taught, preached, and traveled to other villages to preach God's Word and share His love. All too soon, furlough time came, and she had to leave her beloved Bomi Hills.

After deputation, Gladys Robinson returned to Bomi Hills Mission on March 18, 1952, accompanied by Missionary Geneva (Jean) Bailey. It didn't take long to fall back into the routine; however, in early July Gladys was diagnosed with a malignant tumor and had to return to the States for treatment. After unsuccessful treatment and excruciating pain, she passed away on December 10, 1953.[5] A tenacious missionary to Africa had laid down her armor and entered her eternal home.

Pauline Gruse (Church of Jesus Christ 1943 / UPC 1948–1971)

Pauline Gruse began her missionary work in 1943 with the Church of Jesus Christ (a small southern organization). When she arrived, the senior missionaries in Liberia were Aaron and Pearl Holmes at the Zoradee Mission.[6] "During her first furlough, Pauline became a UPC minister and received a UPC appointment to Liberia in 1948."[7] Interestingly, Pauline met the UPC Missions Board in the same meeting in 1948 when E. L. and Nona Freeman received their UPC appointment to South Africa.

While many pioneer missionaries in Liberia left only sparse records or none at all, the essence of their courageous and sacrificial labor has been preserved in Pauline's autobiography, *I Surrender All*. Pauline also provided an insightful account of the callings and sacrificial labors of other single women who served in Liberia. Portions of her life and mission work are recorded here to speak for the women who heeded God's call and labored in primitive conditions, giving their all.

At age eleven, Pauline first heard God's call to missions: "I want you to become a medical missionary!"[8] As she grew older and experienced many disappointments and life challenges, God's call grew fainter and almost forgotten until a door miraculously opened for her to study nursing, reviving the memory of hearing God's voice about medical missions. However, an unwise decision to begin dating while in nurse's training led to marriage, the birth of a son, and then a failed marriage. Though her parents claimed church ties (Methodist and Dunkard), they seldom attended church. Pauline attended church only sporadically until problems arose in her second marriage. At that juncture, she reconnected with a nursing-school friend who had become a Pentecostal. This friend invited her to attend revival services.

This connection with her old friend led her to the Apostolic message and ultimately to baptism in Jesus' name and the infilling of the Holy Ghost. Soon after her conversion, her husband moved out, filed for divorce, and left her destitute. He later returned and threatened her with a gun, but God miraculously protected her. One afternoon while seeking God's direction, Pauline had a vision of the continent of Africa. In the vision, she saw a young girl sitting under a shade tree and again heard the words, "I want you to become a medical missionary!"[9] She felt overwhelmed that God had not given up on the call He had placed on her life some twenty-five years earlier.

Though Pauline felt motivated to find a means to go to Africa, she heeded her pastor's advice to become more involved in the local church ministry. However, she did write a letter to W. T. Witherspoon, general chairman of the Pentecostal Assemblies of Jesus Christ, asking his organization to sponsor her going to Africa. He answered,

"If you are ever able to go to Africa, Sister Gruse, it will be by your faith."[10]

In the following months while ministering in Tennessee, she learned of Apostolic College in Tulsa, Oklahoma, and felt divinely directed to apply for admission. The door opened, and she attended for two years with God's miraculous financial provision.[11] After graduating, Pauline wrote to the director of Foreign Missions for the Church of Jesus Christ, the church with which she held a ministerial license, requesting a missionary appointment. A second letter from the missions director informed her that she had been approved for a three-year appointment. The board would provide her fare to and from Liberia and pay her a salary of fifty dollars per month.

In January 1943, Pauline boarded the *Maritimos* along with Missionary Porter Davis and his wife, and sailed for Liberia.[12] Including the Davises and Pauline, fifteen missionaries sponsored by various missions organizations were on board the ship bound for Liberia.[13]

The trip to Liberia by ship, truck travel in torrential rain, and a short air flight during World War II proved difficult and, at times, dangerous. Pauline began her mission work at the Beajah Mission with the Porter Davises. Travel to Beajah included a four-hour boat trip up the Saint Paul River followed by two days on foot through torrential rain. Pauline wrote, "Here I was, Pauline Gruse, a reasonably intelligent 39-year-old woman, slipping, sliding, and wading ankle deep in mud, swatting the giant Mango flies that swarmed incessantly about my head, all the time fighting with every ounce of strength I had to keep my balance on the narrow, uneven trail."[14] On arrival at Beajah, Pauline moved into a native hut. Her household furnishings consisted of an army cot, a trunk, a makeshift chair, several crude wooden boxes, and mosquito netting. Her work involved teaching, nursing, and weekend visits to preach in other villages.[15]

Pauline was so busy during the first few months at Beajah hopping between teaching and nursing from sunup to sundown that she seldom left the compound. While some of the children were orphans, most had been brought to the mission for feeding, clothing, housing, and education. After about six months, she began preaching in nearby villages.[16]

During her first missionary term with the Church of Jesus Christ, Pauline became a "full-fledged" missionary. Initially, she made short trips to neighboring villages to share the gospel. Then on one of her visits to Monrovia to buy supplies, she met Mildred, a single lady who was affiliated with another Pentecostal organization. Together they made plans to travel to remote villages in the bush in northern and southern Liberia. They mapped out their routes on crude maps left by former missionaries. Their first trip into the north lasted six weeks. Three mission boys and two girls accompanied them, along with carriers. They relied on the generosity of the villages where they overnighted to supply food, but they took along some buckets, dishes, utensils, bedding, and a few changes of clothing as well as an ample supply of coffee, salt, and pepper. They also took army cots, mosquito netting, and two hammock carriers. Initially, Pauline submitted to the practice of the missionary being transported by four carriers on the lengthy treks in the bush.[17]

Within days of their return from the north, Pauline and Mildred headed out on their trek to the south. Since no coastal highway connected the northern coast of Liberia with the southern coast, they hired a motorboat.

Unfortunately, the boat engine failed, leaving them drifting into the Atlantic Ocean. Recognizing the danger, the two ladies began to pray earnestly. Pauline remembered thinking, *How ironic to come as a missionary to the jungles of Liberia, only to drown in the Atlantic Ocean. I could have done this in New York.*[18] Thankfully, their drifting boat was spotted, and they were rescued from the turbulent seas; however, Pauline's seasickness left her exhausted. They were offered a room for the night in Greenville, a city in southern Liberia, before hiring nationals to row them upriver to the Matroe Mission. They spent two weeks at Matroe teaching and providing medical care.[19]

The two ladies left the Matroe Mission and pushed deeper into the bush. They found a warm reception in villages and a request for them to stay: "We beg you not to go. Please . . . our children need you." Yet they felt they needed to move on. After trudging through dense jungles and a flooding river, they arrived at Seabeahta, where Mildred sensed God wanted her to establish a mission. Pauline stayed to help Mildred get settled and begin her work. During these months, as they taught God's Word, they felt led to hold a juju burning (*juju* is a West African term for items that supposedly have magical powers) to emphasize that the Liberians must put their total trust in God. It seemed that the entire village gathered for the bonfire. The village chief himself stepped forward to burn his juju. Even the medicine man threw his juju in the fire. However, the next week, the medicine man brought a small, black, highly polished gourd and gave it to Pauline, admitting that he had held it back.[20]

After more than two months, Pauline left Seabeahta and walked back to the coast to return to Beajah. When she arrived back at the Matroe Mission, she learned that a bush pilot would be flying to Monrovia, and she could fly with him, thus avoiding a boat trip back up the coast. After three days of rest in Monrovia, she returned to Beajah to meet the Pettys, the UPC-appointed missionaries, and began preparing to leave for her furlough. During her absence, the Davises had left for furlough.

Back at the Beajah Mission, Pauline received a letter from the missionary secretary, Wynn Stairs, inviting her to apply for a license with the UPC. She replied, telling him she would give the matter prayerful consideration and get back to him upon her return to the States. After three and a half years in Liberia, Pauline flew back to the States for furlough in 1947.[21]

On her return to Liberia in late 1948 as a UPC-appointed missionary, Pauline moved from the Beajah Mission to the Maheh Mission to work with newly appointed Georgia Regenhardt at the request of the missions board. That same year, the missionaries received a communication from Wynn Stairs, which changed the priorities of the missionaries. He instructed them to begin deemphasizing the mission-school concept, freeing them to evangelize the outlying villages.[22] Until this time, the emphasis in Liberia had focused on establishing village mission schools. Parents would deposit their children at the schools to be educated and cared for daily. Missionaries appointed to Liberia tended to be teachers, often women, who could teach and oversee schools.

In the early part of 1952, Pauline received a letter from Missions Director Stairs assuring her that he was counting on her to establish a new mission in the near future. Pauline's personal account details how God directed her to launch out from Bomi Hills Mission to establish the new mission in a remote area accessible only by walking. With the arrival of a new missionary, Geneva (Jean) Bailey, the adventure into unknown territory began. That account is shared in the following story, which includes Jean Bailey, who was appointed to assist Pauline in establishing the new mission station.[23]

Geneva (Jean) Bailey (1951–1960) and Establishment of Fassama Mission with Pauline Gruse

In 1952, Pauline and Geneva (Jean) Bailey departed from Bomi Hills Mission with the intent to locate a place in the interior of Liberia where the Apostolic message had not yet penetrated. Taking the suggestion of a government officer who served an area in the remote interior, they trekked on foot through the jungle toward Belle country, along with young men carrying their supplies. They took the quickest route, walking some six to ten hours daily. Jean's feet became severely blistered on the second day, and Pauline hired carriers to transport her on the third day. Pauline went on ahead, leaving Jean behind until her feet improved.[24]

Pauline wrote about her frightening walk on the rainy, dark night as she and the carriers, who also seemed afraid, arrived at the village of Belle Yella at 11:00 PM.

> We stopped at the first hut we came to and asked permission to come in out of the rain. . . .
>
> After we had been there a few moments, one of the older boys left in search of the village chief. Chief Weedor emerged from the black night, carrying a lantern and wearing a rubber raincoat that he no doubt had obtained while serving in the Liberian

> army. Walking straight toward me, he stopped just inches from my face and began staring with those dark, piercing eyes that seemed to be looking straight through me. After what seemed like an eternity, he finally broke the silence:
>
> "What did you come here for?"
>
> "I'm a missionary," I explained. "And I've come here to build a mission." There was silence again for several moments as I sucked in my breath, wondering what his next move would be.
>
> "Ma, I'm so glad you have come. We need you to help us."[25]

The chief suggested that Pauline and Jean not settle in Belle Yella. Instead, they opened their mission across the river from Fassama Village, the largest village in Belle country and another six-hour distance from Belle Yella. A decade later, missionary Sam Latta (appointed to Liberia in 1965) described Fassama as sixty-five miles from the nearest motor road—a dirt road—and an hour's flight in a small plane from Bomi Hills.[26]

Working in adverse conditions, Pauline and Jean built the mission compound and school at Fassama. They also pioneered a growing church, seeing converts even among the chief's family. The oldest son and heir of the chief, along with his wife, received the Holy Ghost. Their conversion infuriated the once-friendly chief, and he solicited the Devil Bush Society to oppose the mission work.

As the believers faced demonic opposition, tragedy struck. During a thunderstorm, a bolt of lightning surged through Pauline's body. In the intervening minutes, she felt suspended somewhere between Heaven and earth, looking down on her lifeless body. As she basked in glory, peace, and rest, she heard the voice of the Lord speak to her: "Your work here on earth is not yet done."[27]

Pauline courageously continued her work—sometimes alone for long periods—until she became physically depleted. She spent a total of twenty-eight years in Liberia; however, not without an interruption. A post in *The Evolving World of Foreign Missions* states that Pauline Gruse retired in 1962, feeling it was God's leading for her to retire after twenty years in Liberia.[28] Though she did retire after twenty years (four terms), she reapplied and returned to Liberia in 1965 for a fifth term at age sixty-one.[29]

After her second retirement in 1971, Pauline lived in Monroe, Michigan, and attended the Monroe Apostolic Church. She returned to Liberia in 1981 to visit the people she had worked with for twenty years.[30] Her autobiography, written with Charles Clanton, was published in 1979, approximately two years before her 1981 visit. Although she had Alzheimer's disease in her last years, she still knew her Lord. On the day of her death, she spoke to the care home nurse, saying, "It is time to say goodbye. He's coming for me."[31] She spoke her final words on January 13, 1998, about six months before her ninety-fourth birthday.

Jean Bailey furloughed in August 1960 after her second term in Liberia. Although she was approved for a third term, she felt it was not God's will for her to return to Liberia. After weeks of struggling with a final decision, she reluctantly heeded the voice of God. When she did not return, Pauline Gruse served alone on the Fassama Mission.[32]

Valda Russell (1953–1975)

Valda Russell, a Jamaican, attended Pentecostal Bible Institute (PBI) in Tupelo, Mississippi, before her missionary appointment. Appointed in 1953, Valda first worked at Bomi Hills Mission and later transferred to other locations.[33] The Russell family had evangelized in Jamaica through affiliation with the PAJC long before the merger that created the UPC. Nina "Mother" Russell, Valda's aunt, had influenced the growth of Oneness Pentecostalism in Jamaica. Most likely, Mother Russell's ministry had implanted a burden for missions in the heart of her niece, Valda. Before attending PBI, Valda held an excellent job in Jamaica and also served as a secretary for Missionary Ralph Reynolds.[34]

A 1972 *Global Witness* mentioned Liberian missionaries Valda Russell, the Denzil Boltons, and Ena Hylton experiencing Holy Ghost revival as they pressed into new villages to establish churches. One new church had an attendance of 250, with fourteen new people receiving the Spirit.[35]

When Valda retired in 1975, Liberian President William Tolbert honored her with a certificate stamped with the country's official seal. On this occasion, the president also recognized the Pentecostal work in Liberia and the members of the UPCI missionary board.[36]

Laverne Collins (1954–1955)

Equipped with a university education, Laverne Collins turned her back on the secular field and offered herself as a teacher in the Liberian mission schools. Appointed in September 1954,[37] she arrived in Monrovia on December 17, 1954, welcomed by missionaries Jean Bailey, Valda Russell, and Hubert Parks. After completing all the government paperwork to teach at the mission school, she headed to the Fassama Mission Station on January 31, 1955, to ease Pauline Gruse's heavy workload. Sadly, less than five months later Laverne fell seriously ill with a fever. Alarmed by her deteriorating health, Pauline sent runners to Bomi Hills to inform Missionary Jack Langham. About an hour after the runners left, Laverne breathed her last. While grieving over Laverne's untimely death, Pauline arranged for Laverne's burial near the mission station.

After Laverne's death, a revival broke out at the Fassama Station. Missionaries Jack and Sandra Langham provided words of compassion that became a key part of the revival, remembering that "except a grain of wheat fall to the ground and die, it abideth alone." Laverne Collins's death left a vivid mark on the people of Liberia.[38] Although she taught for only a few months, her dedication to missions produced an abundant harvest.

Else Lund (1962–1971)

Although Else's story is shared earlier in this book, she is mentioned here to identify her chronologically among the eight single women who served in Liberia as appointed missionaries of the UPCI.

Ena Hylton (1963–1973)

Ena Hylton followed in the footsteps of her fellow Jamaican, Valda Russell, in answering God's call to Liberia. Leaving her home in Jamaica in 1960, Ena traveled to Portland, Oregon, and enrolled in Conquerors Bible College, where she studied for three years. While enrolled in Bible college, she felt God's call to missions. Soon after graduating from CBC in 1963, she received her appointment to Liberia and worked with Else Lund as a teacher at Fassama Mission Station under the direction of Pauline Gruse. In 1970, Ena began oversight of the Bomi Hills Mission.[39] In 1972, she moved to Mano River to evangelize a new area.

The two single ladies from Jamaica—Valda and Ena—taught and evangelized in Liberia during the same time frame, although on different mission stations. Valda arrived in Liberia ten years before Ena. After Ena completed ten years as a UPC missionary, she remained in Liberia as an independent missionary.

The history of single women who went to Liberia as teachers reveals that their ministries reached far beyond the classroom. In their love for lost souls, they became significantly involved in evangelizing, preaching, and constructing buildings.

8
East Africa (Kenya, Tanzania, Malawi)

Bobbye Wendell, Darline Kantola (Royer), Loice Sparks

Kenya

Bobbye Wendell (1978–1981)

Bobbye Wendell began her missionary work in Ethiopia as a married woman, wife to Kenneth. (Read the story of the remarkable Ethiopian revival in *SENT! Volume 3, Africa.*) Bobbye had to leave Ethiopia in 1972 with Kenneth and their four children due to extreme political turmoil, but her heart remained in Africa. After the untimely death of her husband and a time of restoration, she applied and received her appointment to Kenya in 1978, where she ministered for three years.

Bobbye made her home in Nairobi, the capital city, where she taught in the Bible school and assisted with the ladies ministry. During Bible school breaks, she traveled to village areas to teach and preach, especially to the Kenyan ladies. During a phone interview at ninety years of age, Bobbye summarized her missionary work in Kenya as "rewarding and pleasant." She found the Kenyan women to be kind, fun, and easy to teach.

In our conversation, Bobbye shared interesting tidbits about preparation for her missionary calling. As a married woman, Bobbye enrolled in Texas Bible College with her husband, Kenneth. At that time, they had two sons, two daughters, and the care of a relative's child. Along with attending TBC and caring for the children, Bobbye drove a school bus to supplement their income. Kenneth began pastoring a church south of Houston, built earlier by Wilma Ruth Nix's father. (See Wilma's story in chapter 10.) The Wendells were classmates at TBC with Wilma, who was appointed to Rhodesia in 1967. Kenneth and Bobbye were appointed to Ethiopia in 1966 while still in Bible college. Following deputation, they arrived in Ethiopia in 1968, and Wilma arrived in Rhodesia in 1969.

In the four decades since Bobbye left Kenya, she has remained active in ministry, preaching and teaching from coast to coast. During one eight-year period, she traveled yearly to Japan to teach in ladies meetings. Many Apostolic believers have remarked that they know Bobbye Wendell or have heard about her ministry. In recent years, she has slowed her pace and enjoys living in her home in Oil City, Louisiana. However, according to Bobbye, she would prefer to be on the road preaching and teaching.[1]

Darline Kantola (Royer), single years 1985–1993

Born and raised by Pentecostal parents in a farmhouse in a mountain valley of Idaho, Darline knew Pentecostal truth at a young age. After being baptized in Jesus' name at age twelve, she sincerely prayed for the Holy Ghost but did not receive the Spirit until two years later at her home church in Donnelly, Idaho. Her parents, Alvin and Tressa Kantola, faithfully attended church and took their girls, Donna and Darline, to district and annual camp meetings. One of Darline's childhood friends was Ferne Scism, whom she met before the Scism family left to begin their missionary service in India. During Ferne's years in India, she corresponded with Darline. This friendship stimulated Darline's interest in missions.

After graduating from high school, Darline debated whether to enroll in Bible college or accept a scholarship to an Idaho college. She felt God's direction to enroll in Conquerors Bible College (CBC). After graduating from CBC, she earned a degree in education and began teaching at Western Apostolic Bible College (now CLC) in Stockton, California. After two years at CLC, she accepted an offer to teach at CBC, where she taught for twenty-three years. During these years, missions remained prominent in her mind, impacted significantly by the teaching of Edwin E. Judd, both at CBC and during his long career in Foreign Missions. Though often feeling drawn to missions, she thought perhaps God's design for her was to teach others who would become missionaries. At one point, more than thirty of her former students were serving on mission fields, and five of the six then-active Foreign Missions regional directors had previously sat in her classroom. Finally, it was time for her to change her classroom location.

After twenty-five years of teaching Bible college in California and Oregon as a single lady, Darline began her missionary years in 1985 as an associate in missions in Kenya. When Darline arrived in Kenya, one of her former students, Tom O'Daniel, became her "boss" since he served as the missionary superintendent of the United Pentecostal Church of Kenya. In 1986, Darline transitioned from AIM to a career missionary appointment.

Along with teaching in the Bible college in Nairobi, Darline traveled frequently to teach in village churches. Flat tires, muddy roads, outdoor toilets, and the inconveniences of country life did not dampen this single lady's missionary enthusiasm. Having been raised in a country setting, she looked forward to traveling and ministering in the rural areas of Kenya.

Her years of singleness ended on June 2, 1990, when she married Arlon Royer, a widowed pastor with adult children from California, in a wedding ceremony in Nairobi, Kenya. That same year, Arlon and Darline received their appointment to Kenya and served there until they were appointed the first UPCI resident missionaries to Uganda in 1993. They retired from missions in 2008. Their missionary years in Kenya and Uganda are summarized in *SENT! Volume 3, Africa.*[2]

After the death of her husband in 2009, Darline resumed overseas teaching as an associated minister with Global Missions. She taught at Harvest Bible College in Glasgow, Scotland, during four different years (2011, 2013, 2014, 2017). Along with intermittent overseas teaching, she has served on the GATS (Global Association of Theological Studies) Curriculum Development Committee and has written books for GATS and Global Missions.

Interestingly, her late husband's son-in-law, John Thomas, now teaches missions classes at Christian Life College, and Darline occasionally joins him in the CLC classroom to share missionary experiences with another generation of potential missionaries. At age eighty-seven, Darline still enjoys teaching and directing young people's vision toward missions.

Tanzania and Malawi

Loice Sparks (1984–1991)

Loice served in Tanzania from May 1984 to January 1989, first as an associate in missions and then as an appointed missionary. After working in Tanzania, Loice moved to Malawi and labored there from January 1989 to December 1991. Due to health conditions, she was not reappointed. In Tanzania, she worked with Missionaries Tim and Carolyn Simoneaux. As a single missionary in Kenya, I enjoyed times of fellowship with Loice and observed her sacrificial dedication to missionary work. Carolyn Simoneaux gladly provided the following summary of Loice's ministry in Tanzania.

> Loice was a pastor and evangelist in Louisiana for thirty-nine years before answering the call to the mission field. She went to Tanzania as an AIMer in the early 1980s, where she served as a furlough replacement for Tim and Carolyn Simoneaux. After completing her AIM assignment, she met the Foreign Missionary Board for an appointment and returned to Tanzania in the mid-1980s as a fully appointed missionary.
>
> Loice worked in the city of Moshi, teaching and preaching in the local churches and teaching at the E. L. Freeman Bible Institute. Additionally, she developed teacher training courses and Sunday school curricula. The Tanzanians lovingly knew her as "Mama Spaki."
>
> Loice dealt bravely with the poor living conditions in Tanzania during her tenure there. Her house had no water source, so she had to have her water trucked in weekly. Electricity was a problem, with power being off more often than on, but her missionary spirit kept her positive and in love with the Tanzanian people. She had a driver who helped her source scarce commodities such as flour, sugar, cooking oil, toilet tissue, and other household

items. Unfortunately, the Tanzanian driver thought he had to have his foot always on the floor to keep the car going. As a result, Loice had to constantly remind him to slow down. She once made him stop at a bad accident scene to observe the results of driving too fast.

Loice was always kind to the Tanzanians and helped them spiritually and materially as much as possible. She was a brave lady who met the challenge of being a missionary with a spirit of dedication and love. Loice passed away in 2006.[3]

9

Central and Southern Africa (Gabon, Lesotho, South Africa)

Colleen Carter, Karen Poole, Neva Russell, Carrie Eastridge

Gabon and Ghana

Colleen Carter (2000–Active)

Colleen Carter followed single women from two previous centuries in her calling to Africa. Near the close of the nineteenth century, Pearl Graham answered God's call to Liberia, West Africa. Many more single ladies heeded God's call to Africa in the early and midtwentieth century. These ladies initially traveled to Africa by ship. God has continued to call as generation after generation of single lady missionaries have completed their years in Africa.

At the dawn of the twenty-first century, a single lady heard God's call to Ghana in West Africa. This missionary traveled by plane rather than an ocean liner as missionaries in the past. Writing the stories of the early single women missionaries involved searching through UPCI missionary records. Compiling the account of Colleen Carter, a current missionary, began with an email to Colleen. Soon after sending the email, I received an iPhone response: "Good afternoon from Ghana!"

Following her greeting, Missionary Colleen Carter shared how God initiated and directed her calling to Ghana. Colleen's first statements reveal the role of parents in a person's calling: "Growing up, the subject of missions was always important in my home, and our house was the missionary 'hotel' and 'restaurant' since we lived in a very small community." At the age of seven, Colleen wrote a Christmas card to Missionaries Everett and Lois Corcoran (Pakistan), and they responded. This birthed an enduring relationship between the seven-year-old and the missionaries.

At age fourteen, Colleen felt a definite call to be a missionary while attending the Whispering Pines Bible Camp in Harcourt, New Brunswick. She remembers turning around from the altar after a time of powerful prayer and saying to her mom, "I'm going to be a missionary." After high school, she studied at Northeast Christian College in Fredericton, New Brunswick, graduating in April 1999. God's plan had begun to unfold even before her graduation.

As it happened, Colleen's brother, Brent, assistant pastor at her church, went to Because of the Times in Alexandria, Louisiana, with Pastor Henry Poitras. While there, Brent and Henry were chatting with Missionary James Poitras (Henry's brother) when James mentioned needing an AIMer in Ghana. At this point, Brent mentioned that his sister, soon to graduate from Bible college, had a call to missions. James quickly handed him his missionary bookmark. When Brent arrived home, he went straight to Colleen's college and gave her the bookmark, which she placed in her Bible.

Colleen's pastor, Arden Bustard, preached on Sunday about following the will of God. Afterward, Colleen took her Bible with the bookmark to the altar, laid her body over it, and prayed, "If this is Your will, God, I will do it and never look back." She called the Poitrases on Monday and began the passport and Associate in Missions application process. She received her AIM appointment to Ghana in April, the month of her graduation.

After Bible college graduation, Colleen moved to Sudbury, Ontario, to live with her aunt and uncle to work and raise funds for her AIM appointment. She worked seventy to seventy-five hours a week on two jobs to raise the needed funding. With finances raised, she flew to Ghana in February 2000 to spend one year with the Poitras family as "an extra set of hands."

Colleen kept her promise to God; she has never looked back. She has served five terms as an associate in missions over a period of seven and a half years. She was appointed an intermediate missionary on September 25, 2007, at the General Conference in Tampa, Florida. After nearly two years of deputation (January 2008–November 2009), she returned to Ghana in February 2010.

Initially, Colleen resided in Accra, where she taught in the Bible college, taught youth and children's seminars, assisted with faculty education, and wrote training materials. Her involvement included preaching and evangelizing. In February 2012, she moved from Accra to the city of Tamale in the northern region to minister in a predominantly Islamic area. No other UPCI missionary had lived outside the capital city. She regards this time as a God-ordained season of her life. While in Tamale, she promoted the building of churches and outreach to new areas.

From June 2014 to March 2015, she deputized again, returning to Ghana in June 2015 as a career missionary. God directed her to move back to Accra in 2017. At this time, Global Missions added regional teaching ministry to her appointment. Colleen has served in multiple capacities: coordinator of Pass the Word printing office, instructor at the African Center for Theological Studies, Sunday school teacher, children's ministry regional coordinator, and secretary/treasurer of the West Africa subregion.

An AIM ministry that started as an extra set of hands for Missionary Linda Poitras in helping with the Poitras girls' schooling developed into a full-fledged teaching and training ministry. As an appointed missionary to Ghana, Colleen spent most of her time in the classroom teaching or in the office preparing the materials to be taught. From her arrival in Ghana in 2000 until 2019, Colleen served faithfully in assisting the missionaries and in devoted ministry with the United Pentecostal Church of Ghana.

In 2019, Colleen's appointment changed to Gabon, where she serves as administrator of the Welch Training Center. Classes began in November 2021 in a new building dedicated to God's glory in February 2022. She ministers in Gabon churches along with her work in the Bible college.

As a single missionary in Gabon, Colleen lives alone in an apartment. In early September 2023, I received a message from Colleen highlighting the unexpected happenings a single missionary may face. She reported that due to the potential turmoil of upcoming elections in Gabon, the internet was sporadic, the airport was closed, and the military had taken over. Colleen was holed up alone in her apartment for safety. She hoped that things would stabilize so the airport would reopen, and she could evacuate to Benin to stay with fellow missionaries. As it turned out, the airport opened, and she flew to Benin, where she participated in the Benin Pastors and Wives Conference and enjoyed the peaceful setting.

Though Gabon faced civil unrest, as is common in many places where missionaries serve, Colleen shared a positive report of God at work. Seventeen people had been baptized in Jesus' name, and three filled with the Spirit. She reported that the Welch Training Center, her center of ministry, had eighteen enrolled students. After nineteen years of missionary experience in Ghana working with a mature and nationalized church, Colleen finds fulfillment in guiding the younger church of Benin through its training and evangelism programs. At the time of this writing, Colleen has spent nearly twenty-four years with UPCI Global Missions, and her story continues![1]

Lesotho

Karen Poole (2021–Active)

Karen's missionary life as a single woman began in October 2021. However, her missionary service officially dates back to 1991 when she and her husband, Robert, became AIMers in Nigeria, West Africa, and also participated in constructing the equipment in Louisiana for the Africa Impact Team. After two terms in Nigeria, Karen and Robert were appointed intermediate missionaries to Cameroon and the Africa Impact Team. The book *SENT! Volume 3, A History of Global Missions, Africa,* recounts their missionary years in West Africa.

The following paragraphs summarize the nineteen years between Robert and Karen's missionary years in Africa as a couple, including Robert's unexpected death during deputation and Karen's appointment as a widowed missionary. I am thankful for Karen's diligence in compiling and sharing the details of her transition from missionary wife to single missionary lady.[2]

In 2002 while on deputation to raise funds to serve in Sierra Leone, the Pooles resigned from Global Missions for the sake of their two girls. They settled in Fayetteville,

North Carolina, near Robert's home church. Five years later, they accepted the pastorate in Beckley, West Virginia, and remained in that capacity for nine years. They then moved to Arizona to care for Robert's mother until her death in 2015.

With their girls raised and the passing of Robert's mother, the Pooles turned their attention to the future. Karen remarked, "Our hearts never left Africa . . . and the Lord led us to apply for reappointment to Sierra Leone in 2016." When they heard that Rusty and Adriane Riddick had just been appointed to Sierra Leone, they broadened their perspective to consider serving in other African countries. Randy Adams, the Africa regional director, mentioned the need for missionaries in Lesotho, so the Pooles agreed to go and were appointed in 2018 as associate missionaries. They arrived on the field in May 2019. They were scheduled to serve in Lesotho for one year to reunite with the people who had been without a missionary for some time. They ministered in each of the churches and taught Bible college classes in two locations.

When the end of their one-year term approached, they found themselves locked in Lesotho due to COVID restrictions. They decided against taking a repatriation flight, since lockdowns were common worldwide. Travel was restricted within Lesotho, so they applied for a special pass, hoping to be able to deliver help to the churches. Their request was denied. The possibility of scarce food supplies was a genuine concern not just for them but for their neighbors in the village just outside the city. The Pooles decided to pray and share what they had if the situation turned dire. As it turned out, their neighbors went to their respective villages, and the area became deserted.

They received word that the Global Missions Board wanted to interview them in June about an upgrade on their appointment. Thus began a five-day ordeal to arrange a flight to Johannesburg to catch a flight back to the United States. Karen referred to this as a complicated "escape from Lesotho" due to the disorganized implementation of COVID restrictions and exceptions. On arrival in Washington, DC, they drove to Florida in a rented car and quarantined there in their RV before flying to St. Louis for the board meeting. They met the board and rejoiced when they were later notified of their appointment as career missionaries to Lesotho. They soon began deputation. However, due to COVID, deputation proved challenging. Some churches were not holding services, others were having online services only, and some were taping interviews with missionaries for later broadcasts.

As they negotiated these deputation challenges, little did Robert and Karen know how COVID would alter their futures. While deputizing in Oregon, Robert began exhibiting symptoms that ultimately led to a COVID-19 diagnosis. After recording a video interview with Pastor Peterson in St. Helens, the Pooles and Petersons went out to eat. As they left the restaurant, Robert was coughing but not feeling too bad. Robert and Karen traveled four hours to North Bend for another deputation service the next day. After the service, Robert told Karen, "I'm really not feeling well." Karen realized it could be COVID-19 and promptly went online and made an appointment with a facility in Oregon City near where their RV was parked. In the morning, Karen drove the four hours to Oregon City. As it turned out, Robert tested positive for COVID-19 and was instructed to quarantine. Although Karen also came down with COVID-19, she recovered without severe complications.

Robert and Karen reflected on recent family losses. Just three and a half months before Robert's diagnosis, his brother, Larry (his only sibling), had died from COVID-19. Since Larry had other health problems, they believed Robert would fare better and focused on prayer and faith. Karen's mother passed away in 2020, just two months after they arrived home from Africa, and Karen didn't even get to see her. They maintained their faith in God, who knows all things and comforts those who mourn.

Karen experienced many frustrations in getting medical help for Robert in Oregon because of state restrictions regarding the treatment of COVID patients. Robert was struggling with a fever, low oxygen levels, and dizziness, but the only "prescriptions" he received were admonitions to wait it out. Desperate to get her husband some help, Karen took Robert to a hospital in Vancouver, Washington. When he was finally attended to, the Pooles were stunned by the nurse's emphatic statement to Karen: "You can't be here! If your husband has COVID, you have to leave!" Karen went to their car, waited, prayed, and cried until Robert was released with prescriptions for two medications.

When she took Robert to the hospital the second time on April 16, 2021, she dropped him off at the door, knowing the medical staff would not let her in. Robert turned, looked at her, and asked, "You're not coming in?" She reminded him that the nurses had kicked her out the previous time. Regrettably, those were the last words that Karen and Robert exchanged face-to-face. He walked into the ER alone while she drove to the parking lot. About an hour later, she received a call notifying her that Robert was being admitted.

Robert spent five weeks and four days in the hospital. During the first week, Karen and their two daughters talked with him by phone. Karen still was not allowed in his room. As the days passed, Robert's breathing became more labored until he could no longer talk. Exactly one week after being admitted. Robert was put into a medically induced coma and placed on a ventilator.

At various times Karen would bring cards and gifts to the hospital and ask if she could see Robert. The answer was always, "No, it's not possible." Karen would leave, choking back tears and sobs.

Karen coped with Robert's sickness in different ways. While they had still been together, she had kept meticulous records of his temperature, oxygen levels, and so on. During his time in the hospital, she still recorded the readings, medications, and doctors' words to monitor his progress until the day he passed. She also spent time outdoors in a nearby park and walking through the neighborhood. She wrote, "Praying and being amongst the birds, trees, and flowers took me away from the struggle and into God's presence."

She felt blessed by the many people God placed in her life during Robert's sickness, beginning with Pastor Gary and Linda Gleason. They and their church furnished meals and loving care. The children and staff of the Oregon City Christian School left cards on her doorstep, letting her know they were praying. Fellow missionaries at the School of Missions (where they were scheduled to be) sent an offering and a big box of goodies. Sending notes of thanks and receiving calls kept Karen's mind from "going down dark roads."

Robert's up-and-down progress was like riding a roller coaster, which created stress in Karen. She believed God for healing but also understood that God was in control. His will would prevail. He knew best.

Although she could not be with her husband, the hospital set up an iPad so she could see and speak to him twice daily via FaceTime. She also put music, stories, and prayers on an old iPod and had the nurses set it up in his room with a small Bluetooth speaker so Robert would be encouraged even while in the coma.

After three weeks, the hospital called Karen to a family care conference to discuss Robert's situation. At her request, Pastor Gleason and Linda accompanied her. The prognosis for Robert was not encouraging. After this meeting, Karen's determination to see her husband intensified. Though repeatedly denied, she finally got an audience with ladies from the Personal Relations office. She was not allowed in the office, but three ladies met with her in the hospital lobby. After a short interchange, one of the ladies said, "We're going to let you in to see him." Karen said she almost fell off her chair! She followed the ladies upstairs to the COVID floor, where they directed her to put on full-body covering before entering her husband's room. She took his hand and whispered, "It's me, Bob; I'm here. They finally let me in." She spent the next three and a half hours with him. His blood pressure and pulse reached better levels during that time. She was allowed to be at his side five times during his last eleven days, including the day he passed. Karen described the day of his passing:

> That fateful day, May 25th, they called me around noon to say Bob's heart was in a critical state, and

> there was a high probability he may not last much longer. I said, "I'm coming!" They responded, "No, don't come yet; we need to get permission first." I answered, "I'm a forty-five-minute drive away, and I'm coming! You can work out the details." I got there, they *did* let me in, and I was with him for his last five and a half hours on this earth.

In talking to Bob in his final hours (although he could not respond), Karen told him she would return to Lesotho to continue their work there if Global Missions saw fit to appoint her. During that time, she continued praying for a miracle until she realized Bob had passed around 7:30. After accepting that Bob was gone, she took down the cards, pictures, and iPod equipment in his room. Then she called their girls and the Gleasons with the news and left the hospital in a state of numbness.

After Robert's passing, Karen consulted separately with her daughters, Rebecca and Jennifer, about their opinions and feelings regarding her desire to return to the mission field. They each responded with the sentiment, "Mom, I would be surprised if you didn't go!"

Karen purchased round-trip tickets from Oregon to their home in Florida, knowing she would need to return to Oregon to sell the motorhome and pack up their belongings. On arrival in Florida, Karen worked with her daughters to plan the memorial service for her beloved Bob.

Pastor John Hopkins III helped facilitate a memorial service that portrayed the congenial Missionary Robert Poole, who enjoyed sharing life's laughter. Out of a desire for attendees to feel comfortable in honoring Robert, Karen invited everyone to feel at home, worship, cry, and laugh. To her delight, the congregation did just that as story after story was shared.

Global Missions Director Bruce Howell spoke last and commented, "I don't know what we're going to do about Lesotho!" In her heart, Karen was responding, "Send me! Send me!" During the meal after the burial, Karen voiced her desire to Director Howell to continue working in Lesotho. He and Global Missions Secretary Scotty Slaydon stated they would work with her to see if that could happen.

After Robert's memorial service, Karen returned to Oregon to sell their motorhome, pack their belongings, and then travel back to Florida in their car. While in Oregon, her car showed signs of significant problems. As it turned out, she had to buy another vehicle, which was an added stress. Thankfully, she found a car that would serve her well on deputation, should she be appointed. With things wrapped up in Oregon, Karen returned to Florida, stopping en route to connect with friends and attend the Louisiana camp meeting.

After Karen arrived in Florida, she was scheduled to meet Africa Regional Director Randy Adams and General Director Bruce Howell and the Global Missions Board about her desire to return to Lesotho. However, her daughter had come down with COVID-19, so she could not keep that appointment in person. Thus, they met via Zoom. During the interchange, she learned two things: (1) she could only apply for an intermediate missionary appointment since she was not an ordained minister; and (2) she must apply for a ministerial license before a missionary appointment could be considered. Learning this, she worked diligently, completed the training, and received her local license.

Karen stepped into the Global Missions Board meeting at the 2021 General Conference for the first time as a single lady. Having met the board with her husband just over a year previously, she knew what to expect. Still, she was grateful that Carolyn Adams, wife of the Africa regional director, had accompanied her to the room. Director Bruce Howell introduced her to the board and made some opening comments. Then he gave Karen an opportunity to address the board. She began by stating, "I know many of you are wondering how this lady who just lost her husband less than six months ago could manage to go back to the mission field by herself."

Karen shared with the board members how she and Robert married late—she at twenty-seven and Robert at thirty-one. Thus, she had lived on her own before marriage. She told how her father, who grew up in a hardscrabble neighborhood, had taught his four daughters (and one son) to be street smart. They knew how to change car tires and oil. He accepted that marriage might not be in his girls' future, and he didn't want them to be stranded or a target for unscrupulous men. When Karen married, she continued to do things independently, even traveling solo or with her children, while Robert continued deputation. She mentioned finances as one of her favorite subjects. At the end of the interview, some of the board members joked about having Karen teach their wives about changing oil and keeping good books. The following week, Karen received notice that her application had been approved. She was thrilled for the opportunity to serve in Lesotho again.

With her appointment approved, Karen began deputation. As she navigated by herself, she gained a new appreciation for all her husband had done to facilitate deputation, such as phone calls to pastors, driving, preaching, and much more. She felt grateful to all the pastors who welcomed her to their churches to present her burden for Lesotho and those who became partners in missions (PIMs). Amazingly, by February 2022, her budget was completed as churches took her on as a partner, and PIMs were transferred to her account when a missionary retired from the field.

Karen took the advice of Global Missions personnel and continued deputation until it was time to attend the School of Missions (SOM) in May. On the Monday following SOM, Karen had her outbound orientation. Eleven days later, on May 20, 2022, Karen boarded a plane to South Africa. A few days less than a year after Robert's death (May 25, 2021), Karen arrived back in Africa. Following her 10:00 PM arrival at the Johannesburg airport, Karen encountered stressful moments navigating the city without a GPS. Thankfully, she made it safely to her scheduled hotel. In summarizing her experience, Karen wrote, "What an introduction to my solo missions' journey on African soil! I knew I had to trust God, that I could trust Him, and He did bring me through without incident."

As Karen began this new journey as a single missionary, she vacillated between a nagging feeling of self-doubt and great confidence when people's words came back to her: "Are you sure you should be doing this?" To such comments, Karen always replied, "Absolutely!"

Now single, however, she came face-to-face with the stark reality of being alone. She had always had Bob's back; now, the decisions were *on her*. She did not doubt the Lord's calling for her return to Lesotho; she just needed to adjust from being the backup to being the one responsible and in charge. Even walking alone in downtown Maseru was a challenge since she had always walked in Bob's shadow of protection. Thankfully, her friend Mme Kabi accompanied her occasionally until she adjusted to life in Lesotho alone.

Karen's neighbor warmly welcomed her back to her house in the compound. He had even hired a cleaning service to dust and tidy up the house. Karen hosted a leadership seminar in her house six days after her arrival. A few weeks later, Karen finally succeeded in accessing church funds to replace a church roof that had been blown off about a year earlier. In August, Karen took three pastors and an interpreter to the Sub-Regional Conference in Zambia. The trip included her driving them to Johannesburg and then flying with them to Zambia. As Karen provided missionary leadership for the church, she found acceptance from the pastors. Before the end of 2022, she had assisted the UPC of Lesotho in locating a suitable property for the Bible school. As of August 2023, the property was paid for. At the time of this writing, Karen is developing building plans and a schedule for starting classes. She considers herself a facilitator, working behind the scenes to help make good things happen for the church in Lesotho. Her goal is to give the church in Lesotho a bright future.

As a single missionary (no longer a missionary wife), Karen commented that she had experienced many firsts: first solo deputation, first solo car purchase from a dealer, first solo overseas flight, first time to drive in the big city of Johannesburg (at night, no less), first time driving eight hours to a mountain village church on "off-roading" tracks, and first time to oversee a large building-repair project.

In her new role as a single minister, Karen had a blessed experience in praying with a woman's daughter to receive the Holy Ghost after a home Bible study. After the closing prayer and the dad had left the house, the daughter wistfully said, "I wish I could get the Holy Ghost! I don't know when it will happen." Karen told her she could receive it right then! Karen then taught a mini-Bible study on receiving the Spirit. Then the daughter's mom and Karen prayed with her. Within a short time, she was inundated with the power and presence of God, speaking fluently in tongues. The mom later received the Holy Ghost, and Karen baptized her dad in Jesus' name—her first time to baptize.

Karen serves under the leadership of Nicky Sisco, area coordinator for South Central Africa. She ministers in the churches, helps organize church repairs, teaches seminars and Bible studies, and serves as the general treasurer. After working alone in Lesotho for nine months, Karen welcomed AIMer Claudia Robinson, whom the Pooles had met in 2019, and Karen had connected with at the 2022 Sub-Regional Conference. Karen stated that Claudia, now an associate missionary, is a tremendous asset to the work. Karen wrote that great things have been happening since her return to the field. Many have been renewed in the Spirit, and new believers have been baptized and filled with the Holy Ghost.

In concluding how she transitioned from being a missionary wife to a single missionary, Karen shared a note she found in Robert's notepad on the first anniversary of his death. Amazingly, she was back in Lesotho—as a single lady missionary.

> *There are many things in this life that parallel the spiritual. One of these is the military. All armed forces that are engaged in warfare have a group that supports and organizes those who are fighting on the front line. A lot of credit goes to those who fight on the front line, but without the rear detachment soldiers, those fighting would quickly be overcome. Therefore, those who are in the rear detachment are equally as important to the success of the mission as those who are sent. Sister, you are as much of a missionary as all those you have helped and supported.*

On that day, Karen wrote: "My husband loved encouraging others; I'm sure this was no exception. I would love to know to whom he wrote this [note], but it was for me today. Yes, I have worked 'on the front lines,' teaching in the Bible school, working in the print shop, teaching Bible studies, etc., but I was also ever his rear detachment. I watched for things he did not see, informed him of things he did not catch in conversation, and made sure he had everything he needed to fulfill his responsibilities, and I was happy to do it all. I am thankful that he was comfortable with me working in both positions. Now I am picking up where we left off, and today he called ME a missionary."[3]

South Africa

Neva Russell (1948)

Neva Russell was listed in the June 1948 *Pentecostal Herald* as an outgoing missionary to South Africa, as noted in *The Evolving World of Foreign Missions.*[4] No additional information about Neva was found.

Carrie Eastridge (1956–1973 / ten years total between these years)

Carrie Lee Powledge Eastridge was born on November 16, 1893, near Macon, Georgia. She married Earl Eastridge in 1915, and they had seven children. Carrie's ill health prompted the family to move to Texas on the recommendation of doctors. The doctors predicted that she had six months to live, but God had other plans. In Texas, a lady invited Carrie to a home prayer meeting where the group prayed for her, and her pain disappeared. In February 1925, Carrie was baptized in the titles Father, Son, and Holy Spirit, and she received the Spirit three months later. She learned about baptism in Jesus' name in June and was rebaptized.[5]

God called Carrie to preach in the adult season of her life as a single mother of six. According to her daughter Nona Freeman, Carrie responded in faith: "Jesus, if you will help me raise my boys, I will preach the gospel no matter what comes, and that she did."[6] In 1935, Carrie began her ministry in Norphlet, Arkansas. During her early ministry years, she built churches in Portales, New Mexico, Raymondville, Texas, and Blackwell, Oklahoma, along with evangelizing in other cities. She later moved to Clovis, New Mexico, where she started a church in a barbershop.[7] While serving in these places as a home missionary in America, she sensed God's call to global missions.

While many Oneness believers are familiar with the names of pioneer missionaries E. L. and Nona Freeman, fewer know that Nona's mother, Carrie Eastridge, served as a missionary in South Africa in her senior years. Carrie's commitment to reaching the lost proved itself in her many years of ministry to Native Americans in North American. Known as "the Builder," she ministered in New Mexico, Texas, Oklahoma, and Wyoming. In 1947, she moved to Indian Village near Gallup, New Mexico, and opened a mission among the Navajo people.[8] Her ministry to the Navajo has continued for many decades through the ministries of her son Jerry and grandsons.

At age sixty-three in 1956, Carrie sold all her earthly possessions and applied to go to South Africa as a foreign missionary, where her daughter Nona and her family served as missionaries. Carrie was denied appointment and was advised to let younger people go. She asked, "'Are any younger men applying?' When told no, she went."[9] She packed her bags and moved on her own to help the Freemans.

Upon receiving a letter from Carrie Eastridge after her arrival in South Africa, the missions board agreed she should apply for missionary appointment. E. L. Freeman wrote a letter to the missionary board requesting that Carrie be appointed while remaining in South Africa, and the board recommended her for appointment on the merits of her "solid-gold reputation."[10] She spent over eight years in Africa (1956–1964) before leaving due to illness. However, she recuperated and later returned.

Carrie was a remarkable preacher and builder. "She did a tremendous work, building beautiful church buildings in Durban, South Africa, and Umtata, Transkei."[11] Missionary news from 1960 stated that "Carrie Eastridge extended the work in South Africa to the Hindus and Mohammedans [Muslims]."[12]

When Carrie returned to the States in 1964 due to poor health, she began traveling among the Navajo people. She preached, taught Bible studies, and prayed for the sick. She was often accompanied by her grandson, Martin Eastridge. By 1969, the Navajo Nation granted a mission-site lease to the UPC, and the Texico District Home Missions department financed a church building in Tohatchi, New Mexico. Although her work among the Navajo was progressing, Carrie longed to return to Africa. Thus, her son Jerry took over the work, and Carrie returned to South Africa in 1971, just after her seventy-eighth birthday, to complete her ten years as a global missionary.[13]

This faithful servant returned to the States in 1973 just in time to celebrate her eightieth birthday with family. Nothing seemed too hard for this self-sacrificing lady who joyfully invested her time and finances into the work of the Kingdom. Carrie continued working for the Lord for eight more years after returning to the States. At age eighty-eight, she preached her last sermon on December 13, 1981, and died ten days later on December 23. Her tombstone inscription states, "I've moved to my new home, but His truth is marching on."

10

Zimbabwe and Bophuthatswana

Wilma Ruth Nix

Planting the Church in Rhodesia (Zimbabwe)

Wilma Ruth Nix (1967–1996)

Wilma Ruth Nix holds a unique and honored role in UPC missionary history. As a single lady, Wilma Ruth courageously founded the UPC in two countries of Africa: Rhodesia (now Zimbabwe) and Bophuthatswana. Appointed in 1967 to Rhodesia at age thirty-four, she served there for twenty years. According to the *1971 Foreign Field Status Report*, she arrived on the field in April 1969. By 1971, she had established five churches with two outstations. Regular attendance totaled 175. She reported sixty-five filled with the Holy Ghost and 109 baptized in Jesus' name. Twenty students attended a twenty-six-week Workers' Training Program held four hours weekly. Four nationals entered the ministry in the year preceding the 1971 report: one general licensed preacher, a local licensed preacher, and two with worker's certificates. Rhodesia was administered with South Africa under Superintendent E. L. Freeman because of the similarity and closeness of the works.

The *1984 Foreign Missions Story*, compiled during Wilma's fourth term in Zimbabwe, shows that Wilma's leadership was productive both spiritually and physically. Two lovely church buildings had been erected in Bulawayo. One was uniquely patterned after the ancient ruins that gave the country its name. Additionally, the UPC of Zimbabwe had an outreach church building and several preaching points. Wilma's father and stepmother, Dewey and Marie Nix, assisted her with building programs, outreach, and the Bible school. Her cousin, William Nix, superintendent of the Michigan District, was a great help in supporting her missionary work.[1]

After twenty years in Zimbabwe, Wilma Ruth felt directed to take the Apostolic message to an additional African country. In May 1988, she moved to Mafikeng, Bophuthatswana, and founded the UPC of Bophuthatswana. On August 17, 1996, a beautiful new church building in Mafikeng was dedicated by Pastor L. E. Westberg from Kansas. Along with church planting, Wilma also established a Bible school.[2]

Only three months after the dedication of the church in Mafikeng, Wilma met an untimely death. She had traveled to Johannesburg and was returning to Mafikeng on November 1 when she was seriously injured in a car accident and was life-flighted to one of Johannesburg's best medical facilities for treatment. Sadly, she passed away three weeks later on November 22. At the time of her death the UPC of Bophuthatswana had grown to five congregations. Her funeral service was held in the newly dedicated building in Mafikeng on November 27, 1996. A second service in Houston, Texas, on November 30 honored her as a valiant soldier of Jesus Christ.

Wilma Ruth Nix began her missionary work in her midthirties following her 1967 appointment. While summarizing her story in *SENT! Volume 3, A History of UPCI Global Missions, Africa*, I found limited information about her twenty-nine years of missionary service. While fellow missionaries in Africa knew about her service, the

UPCI fellowship had limited awareness of her pioneer ministry.

After completing the Africa story, I learned that Lesley Kelley, who lives in California about eighty miles from me, was converted as a ten-year-old child under Wilma Ruth's teaching in Rhodesia (later known as Zimbabwe) and grew to adulthood under her spiritual mentorship. As a young adult, Lesley became a coworker with Wilma in Zimbabwe as well as Bophuthatswana. She served with Wilma until Wilma's tragic death, remaining in Bophuthatswana for a season to continue the work Wilma Ruth had begun. In God's providence, Lesley ultimately married Michael Kelley, an American preacher whom Lesley had met while Michael was serving in Africa in short-term missions. The following content is an edited version of Lesley's firsthand account of Wilma Ruth and her missionary work.

It was just an ordinary Saturday afternoon in the balmy winter of 1971 in Bulawayo, Rhodesia (now Zimbabwe), when a knock on my family's front door changed our lives, mine especially. And so the story of my life with missionary Wilma Ruth Nix from Texas, USA, began. She had come to our home to introduce herself after my twelve-year-old brother had visited Sunday school with a friend. She was absolutely charming, and she was thrilled that there were other children in the home she could invite to Sunday school. At that time, I was ten years old and excited to attend Sunday school. I can honestly say that one Sunday school visitation from Missionary Nix became my saving grace and later that of my family.

This wonderful woman of God was dynamite packed into a tiny human frame. So many times, I have looked back in awe with the thought, "Dear God, I am here today serving You because one woman stepped out on a calling from You that many would not have heeded!" I am beyond humbled.

Wilma Ruth Nix was born an only child to Dewey and Gertrude Nix in Texas on September 19, 1932. She was raised in a godly, prayer-nurtured home, which instilled strong work and moral ethics in her. She was influenced by many ministers of the gospel, including a missionary who served in South America. While still a teenage schoolgirl, she worked an after-school job and began preaching.

When Wilma Ruth was only two months old, God told her mother that Wilma Ruth would be a missionary one day. Wilma's mother held that secret in her heart until just before her death. When her mother shared this knowledge, plans were already underway for Wilma to go to the mission field. Sadly, her mother passed away before Wilma became a missionary. Her wise mother wanted to assure Wilma that her calling was from God and God alone.

Wilma Ruth's own words verify God's calling:

> At the age of fourteen, God visited me during the night and many days following and let me know that I would go to Africa. Just how or when, I did not know. While we were having a tent revival in Rosenberg, I came out from under the tent after praying alone, and I saw the name of a city in the sky. I did not know how to pronounce it, but it started with a "B." After searching a world map for some time and not finding it, I left it in the hands of the Lord but never forgot it. Only years later would I understand how God was going to fit the puzzle together. On the Texas Bible College campus, God directed me more and more toward missions. I was the Missions Club president for one year and then

> became the advisor during my last year when I was teaching Missions and Bible Geography at the college. During that year, as I was praying in my apartment, an audible voice spoke "Rhodesia" to me. Oscar Vouga (director of Foreign Missions) was on the campus a few days later, and I asked him what the possibilities were for me to go to Rhodesia. He asked, "Which one?" I didn't know there was more than one Rhodesia, so I was very puzzled. Why didn't God tell me which one? Bobbye Wendell, who wanted to go to Ethiopia, went with me to the public library in downtown Houston. When I asked the librarian if there were two Rhodesias, she answered no. Northern Rhodesia had become Zambia that year, so there was now only one Rhodesia. God keeps up with current events. Praise the Lord!

Wilma met the UPC Missions Board in 1967. Because she was a single woman, they felt concerned for her. Rhodesia had its woes. Terrorists had begun to infiltrate Rhodesia in 1966, mainly through Zambia, attacking the farms and villages. The ongoing attacks escalated into the horrific Bush War that lasted for thirteen years. During the war, sanctions were placed on landlocked Rhodesia. The nation thrived despite the fuel and food rationing due to the sanctions. Though the Foreign Missions Board felt concerned for Wilma Ruth as a single lady, they recognized her calling and granted her an appointment.

Missionaries E. L. and Nona Freeman traveled from South Africa to "spy out the land" before Wilma's arrival. They reported that there was an open door for her in Bulawayo. Mention of the name Bulawayo resonated with Wilma. It was the name she had seen in the sky several years before, starting with the letter B. She had finally found the city to which God had called her.

On April 20, 1969, Wilma Ruth stepped onto Rhodesian soil. According to the Freemans, God performed a miracle, directing the new missionary to open three churches within three months. Wilma expressed that she had not visualized such a beginning in the beautiful country that captured her heart.

Her own words provide a glimpse of her missionary years. "I was personally responsible for thirteen services each week. The words 'Go forward, slack not' were my motto. My first term was five years, and I loved every minute of it. I must say it was tremendous when the Lord gave workers to share the load. My dad was very busy building the Metopos Road Church and preaching as much as he could."

Dewey and Marie Nix, her father and stepmother, came to Rhodesia for a season to help establish the church. Their work proved invaluable. The St. John's Ambulance Hall in Famona, where services were initially held, became too small for the growing congregation, and there were no rooms for Sunday school classes although they still taught the children. The hall often had to be cleaned because of the previous night's functions. The new church building provided rooms for teaching the children more effectively. I, Lesley Kelley, was one of those children.

Both Wilma Ruth and Marie Nix reminded us children that we needed to be baptized in Jesus' name and filled with the Holy Ghost to be saved. I recall that our Sunday school class had a "tarry meeting" on October 2, 1973. Louis Louw, a young man who later became a missionary to Namibia, was one of the teachers. That night I and another child received the Holy Ghost. Wilma Ruth gave special attention to teaching children and leading them to salvation.

Wilma Ruth searched for property for the growing church and found a prime piece on the corner of Edenhall and Metopos Roads. She knew this was where God wanted her to build the church. Though a high underground water table presented challenges, she and her father forged ahead with construction. The Metopos Road United Pentecostal Church of Rhodesia was dedicated on August 9, 1974. It stands as a testament to the glory of God. Pastor C. L. Dees, Wilma Ruth's pastor in Texas, came as the guest speaker for the church dedication. The Sunday newspaper in Bulawayo featured this magnificent church building in its June 9, 1974, issue, giving the church great advertisement. The unique building featured a chevron design (an inverted V pattern creating a zig-zag design) in brick inspired by the ancient Zimbabwe ruins. Interestingly, the country's name changed from Rhodesia to Zimbabwe in six years.

The newspaper printed this description: "Outside, the circular building sweeps up to a 15m triangular tower to be glassed on one side. Inside is a web of unroofed passages along the outer wall; arches and platforms at different levels, and a 'sunray' spread of beams forming the ceiling of the auditorium or sanctuary. . . . When finished, the church will cost between $30,000 and $40,000 as built by Rev. Nix and his limited African labour. A contractor's price these days would be nearer $90,000, the pastor said last week."

Wilma Ruth involved the church people in raising funds for the building project. They held bake sales, conducted auctions, and sponsored twenty-kilometer walks. The young converts found these activities fun and exciting. As one of the converts, I look back in awe at how this single missionary lady had such vision, passion, and drive for the work of God. Stalwart and faithful, she never slackened her pace in preaching the gospel and never considered returning to America.

Wilma Ruth focused on nurturing strong national leaders, pastors, evangelists, outpost preaching points, churches, and godly saints. She invited many North American visitors to help strengthen and equip the church. She kept mentors in her life, particularly Pastor William Nix (her cousin) and his wife, Candace, of Ypsilanti, Michigan, and her Texas pastor, C. L. Dees. She turned to them for prayer and wisdom. The church grew rapidly, with prayer and fasting as priorities. Prayer service convened from 5:00 to 7:00 PM every Saturday at the church. All-night prayer meetings were held periodically, with people coming to pray at two-hour intervals.

Wilma Ruth became the first woman in Rhodesia to become a marriage officer. The announcement of this appointment in the *Sunday News* gave her added recognition in Bulawayo. She officiated her first wedding at the Metopos Road Church before it was completed. Numerous weddings followed over the years.

Along with church planting, Wilma Ruth established Whole Truth Bible College (WTBC). I was privileged to graduate from WTBC with my BA in Theology. UPCI General Superintendent Nathaniel Urshan ministered at my graduation. The college was kept on par with Texas Bible College curricula and standards. Wilma Ruth's excellence as a student at TBC had prepared her for Bible college ministry. A story was told that a TBC instructor gave an extremely hard test, and most students failed it. The instructor acknowledged he would know if the test was too hard and would redo it if Wilma Ruth did not get an A on the test. She did not! The students felt relieved. Wilma Ruth's meticulous instructions about Bible study have stuck with me to this day.

Wilma Ruth was a trailblazer. Despite the terrors of the Bush War, she continued reaching into the townships. She would pack her Sheaves for Christ (SFC) Toyota Cressida station wagon with gospel workers and take off to preach and teach God's Word. In the process, she developed loyal and dedicated ministers. At one point, she purchased a large piece of property with a farmhouse just outside the town of QueQue (now KweKwe), surrounded by the African bush. A house and the foundation for a large tabernacle were built, and then services began under the open night skies, often continuing late into the night and wee hours of the morning. Some of us would fall asleep listening to the singing and the fervent prayers.

In 1980, Rhodesia became Zimbabwe. As Wilma Ruth continued her travels, she was no longer a newcomer in many places. I remember traveling with her to one of the township church buildings. People walking along the dusty road toward church waved and smiled as we drove past in the SFC car packed with people. On arrival at the church, I sat in the front row. People squeezed in front to sit on the floor. As more came, the floor-sitting crowd extended forward and onto the platform. I don't recall how many responded that night to the preaching. Still, I remain impressed that a single lady missionary faced inconveniences as she faithfully traveled to spread truth in Zimbabwe.

During Wilma Ruth's years in Zimbabwe, Dorothy Edwards, a bubbly single lady from Ohio, came to South Africa in the early 1970s for a season, and visited

Rhodesia. As it turned out, she quickly became immersed in the work in Rhodesia and ultimately stayed on with the Nixes. She became widely known as Sister Dot. Engaged in the work, she bought her own home and became a tremendous help. When Wilma Ruth left Zimbabwe, Dorothy effectively directed the work of the Bible college. Africa became her permanent home. Though she never sought an official appointment as a missionary, she did receive an AIM appointment while in Zimbabwe. Records show that she was in South Africa in 1974 (with no note of when she went there), and in 1975 she went from South Africa to Zimbabwe (Rhodesia). She passed away in 2014.[3]

Planting the Church in Bophuthatswana

Lesley Kelley continued her narrative:

After twenty years of planting, watering, and harvesting in Rhodesia (Zimbabwe), Wilma Ruth responded to God's call to Bophuthatswana, a country just south of Zimbabwe. In her fifty-fifth year, Wilma heard God's voice to "pick up her sickle" and move south. Donald and Sharon Ikerd (missionaries in South Africa) traveled with her to Mafikeng to locate a house and find a place to hold church services. While house hunting, their car failed to start. As they pushed it to the roadside, a man pulled up on his motorbike and invited them to push it into his nearby yard. Then his wife invited them to a steak dinner she was preparing. As Wilma Ruth shared her vision and need for a building, the host informed them that he was the very man who could assist them in signing a lease on the MOTH Hall in the center of town. A divine appointment! After dinner, the men went to the car to assess the problem. Inexplicably, the car started immediately.

Wilma Ruth began services without delay. The only attendees were Wilma Ruth, AIMer Cindi Osborne, the hall caretaker (who was usually inebriated), and me. Cindi, a talented musician, led the singing before Wilma Ruth preached. I had moved with Wilma from Zimbabwe to work with the youth and Sunday school. Attendance increased quickly.

Wilma Ruth connected easily with strangers. While standing in line at a store, she would smile at a person nearby and kindly ask, "Have we met before?" Or sweetly ask, "Do I know you?" or something similar. "No, I don't believe so," would be the usual response. That exchange would open a door, and she would introduce herself and tell them about the church with a warm invitation to be her guest the following Sunday. Wilma Ruth kept home-made cake on hand for the many visitors she invited for "tea." She did not like tea but desired to reach the lost at any cost. So she became all things to all people so that she might win some to God. Her friendly smile, her connection to people, and her burden brought many to church and ultimately to salvation. The Mafikeng Public Swimming Pool served as the first baptistery. The first two converts were baptized by visiting minister William Nix, her cousin.

Wilma Ruth's work deserves a book of its own. She organized crusades, directed conferences, conducted Sunday school and youth services, counseled, and gave home Bible studies. Some of the converts from Zimbabwe who had moved to South Africa reconnected with her, and a few moved to Bophuthatswana to help establish the work.

In 1993, she opened a Bible school in Mafikeng to train men and women for spiritual leadership. Over time, six daughter works were opened in surrounding areas.

I traveled with her down dusty dirt roads, often looking for a particular shack, signage, or landmark to locate a group where she was scheduled to minister. Commonly, barefoot children ran alongside our slow-moving car, waving, smiling, and dancing as we listened for the sound of worshipers.

In one youth service, she challenged the attendees with this poem about Teenage Dreams:

> *It's not enough to have a dream unless I'm willing to pursue it.*
> *It's not enough to know what's right unless I'm strong enough to do it.*
> *It's not enough to join the crowd, to be acknowledged and accepted.*
> *I must be true to my ideals, even if I am left out and rejected.*
> *It's not enough to learn the truth unless I also learn to live it.*
> *It's not enough to reach for love unless I care enough to give it.*
> *– Author unknown*

In August 1996, the completion of another beautiful church building testified to Wilma Ruth's steadfast labor. Pastor Westberg from Kansas was the speaker for the dedication, a time of great rejoicing. Three months later, Wilma Ruth completed her mission at age sixty-four. God called her to her eternal reward on November 22, 1996, following a vehicle accident from which she did not recover. A beautiful memorial service was held at the recently dedicated building in Mafikeng and another at Pastor Kilgore's church in Houston, Texas. She was laid to rest in the countryside cemetery in Livingston, Texas, where her parents were buried.

In conclusion, I quote from Wilma's notes: "If there be any praise, if there be any glory, let it all go to Jesus Christ, who was the author of it all."[4]

PART III
NORTH & CENTRAL AMERICA

11

Alaska

Before Statehood

Grace Yadon (Wiens), single years 1947–1949

Frank and Hattie Yadon welcomed their second daughter, Grace, to their Idaho home on February 9, 1924. She joined her six older siblings, Emmett, Haskell, Paul, Evangeline, Frank, and Charlie. Their first-born daughter, Evangeline, had met a tragic death at age ten when she was hit by a car on returning home from Sunday school. Another brother, Johnny, who followed Grace, passed away at age two. Thus, Grace remained an honored sister of her five older brothers. Born to parents who had received their personal Pentecost as a young couple, Grace grew up influenced by Spirit-filled parents. The Yadons' remarkable conversion story is told in *Unto You and Your Children* by Grace Yadon Wiens.[1]

Desiring to be a fruitful servant of God, Grace studied with her brother Charlie at the Pentecostal Bible Institute (PBI) in Tupelo, Mississippi. Before attending Bible college, Grace and Charlie had evangelized in the Midwest, South, and Northwest.

In September 1947, after graduating from PBI, Grace and Charlie went to Sitka, Alaska, to assist pioneer missionaries Kenneth and Louise French. Their initial plan to spend six weeks in outreach in villages and canneries extended to two years. Grace and Charlie rented a house in the village of Hoonah on the northern shore of Chichagof Island in November 1947 and began church services. Initially, attendees were primarily children. However, the faithful labors of this brother-sister team planted a permanent church. At the time of this writing, seventy-six years later, the United Pentecostal Church continues in Hoonah.

According to Foreign Missions records, Grace initially worked in Alaska without a missionary appointment.[2] In the early days of the UPC, single women seldom received a missionary appointment. However, her ministry in Alaska apparently gained the confidence of board members. The October 1947 minutes of the Foreign Missions Board meeting state that Grace Yadon was recommended for appointment, and in 1948, she was listed as a missionary "on the field."[3] The January 1949 Foreign Missions Board minutes recommended that she stay in Alaska,[4] and her name appeared on the "1949 Missionary Listing."[5]

In 1948, Charlie returned to the Lower 48 to marry a young lady named Orpha, whom he had loved since age sixteen. Grace remained in Hoonah as a single lady missionary to continue leading the church they had started. Grace's son, Ed Wiens, told me that his mother spoke about the darkness she sometimes experienced in ministering where evil spirits were prevalent.

In April 1949, her life's course changed. Grace wrote in her unpublished booklet, *One Room Cabin*, "I flew out of Hoonah on the Alaska Coastal seaplane and then took a big plane from Juneau to Seattle. My friends, the McGrews, drove me to Grandview in time to attend Charlie and Orpha's lovely wedding. Charlie was surprised to see me as I hadn't told him I was coming."[6]

After the wedding, Charlie and his bride returned to Hoonah, and Grace went to her parents' home in Rock Creek Canyon near Kimberly, Idaho. However, Grace did not settle down in Idaho for an extended time. On November 15, 1949, she married David Wiens, and he took her back to Alaska. Grace wrote, "Returning to Southeast Alaska in 1950 in our first year of marriage filled me with joy to be back among 'my native people.'" In 1952, David and Grace were appointed as missionaries to Alaska.[7] About a decade later, in 1963, they were appointed to Peru.

In conversing with Grace's son, Ed Wiens, I was reminded that Grace had felt a definite call to Africa. However, she was informed that a single lady would not be given a missionary appointment. Interestingly, her calling to reach souls took her to Native Alaskans and eventually resulted in her appointment as a missionary.

Knowing of his mother's lifelong heart for the people of Africa, Ed took his mother to Nigeria in 2010 when she was eighty-six. Six years after her trip to Africa, Grace took a final flight to her eternal abode on May 29, 2016. In her last days, she wrote a message, tucked it in an envelope, and instructed it was not to be opened until her memorial service, where she wanted it read. Her son Ed had the responsibility and honor to read his mother's last words to those who came to honor her.

Grace's last words, recorded on a six-page, single-spaced manuscript, contained loving words of wisdom, instruction, and encouragement to the living. She pointedly addressed family members, young men, young women, married couples, and preachers, prefaced by this statement: "I couldn't leave this life without a few words of encouragement and help. . . . I would never call it 'advice,' so don't hunker down and hide." Grace envisioned her abode in Heaven:

> Missionaries from around the world are surrounded by people of all tribes and tongues. . . .

> They took the gospel of Good News to them, some ages ago, before airplanes. Happiness and joy radiate all over Heaven. You can't believe the dancing and laughing. I'm even "running the aisles" on the golden streets! On earth, I always wanted to find a gold nugget, but here I am, walking all over the stuff. No pious starch up here! I'm not even winded!

I can verify that Grace was given a fitting name by her parents, Frank and Hattie Yadon. She radiated God's love and grace as she ministered publicly and personally. When I was a teenager, David and Grace Wiens pastored my home church in Donnelly, Idaho. Grace brightened my days with wise and witty wisdom through the years when our paths crossed. During my years as a Bible college teacher in Oregon, I enjoyed teaching two of her children, Ed and Jolene, who assisted me in compiling Grace's story for this book. I am confident that many more young women like Grace will hear and heed God's call to global missions. Heeding God's call to missions may begin singly, but it may lead to marital partnership in God's time.

12

El Salvador, Honduras, and Belize

Cathy Killoren and Amy Sawyer

El Salvador

Cathy Killoren (1989–2007)

Cathy began her life's journey in St. Louis, Missouri, on April 19, 1955, as the newborn daughter of Thomas M. Killoren and Margie W. Hewell. She ended her life's journey in El Salvador on November 28, 2007, while serving as a missionary.

After Cathy committed her life to the Lord, she studied theology at Jackson College of Ministries in Mississippi, graduating with high honors. She also won the Jacksonian Award as an outstanding graduate. After graduation, she joined the staff at First Pentecostal Church in Jackson, Mississippi, although her home was in La Grange, Georgia. While serving in Jackson, she received her calling to the country of El Salvador.

Cathy began her missionary work in May 1989 with the Associates in Missions (AIM) program of the UPCI. Her dedication and love for the Salvadoran people led to her 1995 appointment as an intermediate missionary to El Salvador. Cathy served in El Salvador along with the Howells and Slaydons. She dedicated her life to ministering to the rich and poor through small groups, Sunday school, medical-missions evangelism, and Bible studies. Cathy was instrumental in founding the medical clinic and spent much time working there.

When she returned to the field after her first furlough, she shared these comments with Global Missions:

"I thought I loved the work here in El Salvador five years ago when I first started, but it is nothing compared to how much I love the people and the work here now. I cannot even imagine spending my life anywhere else."[1]

As Cathy's ministry progressed, she received ordination as a UPCI minister, followed by her appointment as a career missionary in 2005. She devoted a total of eighteen years to missionary ministry. Sadly, Cathy passed away on the field on November 28, 2007. She never lost her love for the people and work where she desired to spend her life. Friends, family, and acquaintances remember her as one who cared for people above everything else.

Amy Sawyer (1989–2020)

When I inquired about Amy's missionary calling and ministry, she kindly agreed to write her story. Firsthand accounts offer insights that other writers cannot replicate. So I thank Amy for sharing how God led her into missionary service and enabled her on the field. With editorial adaptations and Amy's approval, here is her story:

I grew up in a home with a dad who had received a call to global missions at ten years of age. Because of this, missions and missionaries were highly regarded in the Sawyer home. We all read every book written by missionaries that we could find and listened to any missionary preaching available to us. We even carried our old tape recorders to the church to record the missionaries' presentations. As a result, from as far back as I can remember, I always desired to serve as a global missionary. As the years passed, I began to feel that desire transition into a call to serve.

As my relationship with the Lord grew in my teenage years, I began to sense a definite missionary calling.

Initially, I did not feel called to a specific country, but I remember the Lord talking to me about my willingness to go where I didn't want to go. When I was about fifteen, I read a book at bedtime by a missionary to Colombia (either Sallie Morley or Mollie Thompson). Before falling asleep, I read about big spiders crawling over the lady missionary. My mind and heart said, "I'm never going to go somewhere like that!" After turning out my light, I could not fall asleep. Over and over, I kept hearing the Lord say, "What if I ask you to go somewhere like that, Amy?" I kept responding, "There are so many other places I can go." The Lord kept repeating the same thing to me, reminding me that I had said I would go anywhere He asked.

As the wakeful hours passed, I got up, knelt beside the bed, and prayed. I repented and told the Lord I would go anywhere He asked, even where I might be afraid to go. I knew that if He protected the missionaries in Colombia, He would protect me too. When I got back into bed, I fell asleep within minutes. I felt like the Lord said that was all He wanted from me: just to be willing. Ironically, when I eventually went to the mission field, I went to El Salvador when the country was in the middle of a civil war. Curfew still existed when I arrived because a significant offensive had just occurred in the city. In every turbulent time, the Lord protected me, even when a battle occurred close to my apartment.

AIM in El Salvador

After high school, I attended Jackson College of Ministries, where I studied and graduated as a missions major. While there, I made my first missions trip to El Salvador, led by Gordon Mallory. My second missions trip during JCM days took me to Guatemala. I felt the Lord begin to talk to me about going to El Salvador. After graduating in November 1989, I applied for AIM to El Salvador. My application was initially denied because Global Missions had just appointed Scotty Slaydon, Cathy Killoren, and a married couple as AIMers to El Salvador. They felt that Missionaries Bruce and Diane Howell would be overloaded with AIMers. Then Brother Howell called, explaining they had a specific job description for me. Thus, Global Missions reversed its decision. I arrived in El Salvador seven months after my Bible college graduation. As an AIMer, I primarily taught ESL (English as a Second Language) in the primary school until I learned to speak Spanish. After learning Spanish, I began teaching Sunday school and working in children's ministry. I remained in El Salvador for about three and a half years, from 1989 to 1993.

AIM in Honduras and Belize

In late 1993, my AIM appointment changed to the country of Honduras. My parents, Jerry and Brenda Sawyer, had been appointed to Honduras at the 1989 General Conference. For the first time I began working in the Bible school. Bruce Howell trained me to do the administrative side of the work, and I started teaching. That's when I found my passion for teaching in Bible school. As an AIMer in Honduras, I assisted in founding the National Youth Department and founded the National Sunday School Department. While youth ministry and Sunday school had operated in some churches before this, no programs had existed on the national level. I spent about five years in Honduras on AIM from 1993 to 1998.

During my last year in Honduras, the Lord began to speak to me about moving to another country. I wasn't sure where, but I assumed it would be a Spanish-speaking country since I had become fluent in the language. I prayed about every Spanish-speaking country globally but felt like the Lord was saying no each time. At about this same time, the Global Missions Board had asked my dad to consider adding Belize to his appointment. They asked him to visit the country and meet some of the pastors before he made his final decision.

I had not prayed about going to Belize because I knew Belize was an English-speaking country. I had never been to Belize, so I asked my parents if I could accompany them on their trip. Since I was personally paying for the trip, I didn't mention my visit to Belize to anyone. I was a bit nervous when I learned that our regional director, Lloyd Shirley, would meet us at the airport. When we exited the airport, Brother Shirley said, "Amy, I'm so glad you came with your parents! Brother Scism has asked me to ask you to come to Belize with your parents and start a Bible school." Once I returned to Honduras and started praying about Belize, the Lord immediately spoke and confirmed that He wanted me to go to Belize. He told me that was why every time I had prayed about a specific country, He had always said, "No, not there." In mid-1998, my AIM appointment was changed to Belize. I arrived in the country the day after my thirtieth birthday. Before going to Belize on AIM, I applied for a UPCI local license, which I received after I arrived in Belize.

Belize was a major change for me. Although it is on the Central American mainland, it is very much a Caribbean country. It is a country of multiple people groups, each having its own culture, language, and religion. I drove from the United States down to Belize with Missionary Johnny Willhoite and his wife, who were going as furlough replacements for three months. However, after eight days in the country, Johnny had a massive heart attack and died. When his wife returned to the States, I remained alone in the country for eight months until my parents arrived.

At that time, the church had eleven ministers and nine churches—one English-speaking and one Spanish-speaking church in the city, plus seven Kekchi Mayan churches deep in the jungle. The pastors of the city churches were a father and son-in-law. A few months later, they resigned from their churches on the same weekend. Since there were no other ministers in the city, I immediately became the pastor of both churches. Two months later, I enthusiastically turned the pastoral role over to my dad on his arrival in the country.

Once I settled in Belize after Johnny Willhoite's death, I began holding evening Bible school classes and reopened a preaching point in a village near the capital city. In the year 2000, I was upgraded to a UPCI general ministerial license.

Within about a year, I opened a traditional Bible school. Unfortunately, this typical campus-style Bible school did not work for the Belizean church. The churches were mainly among the Mayan Indians at the time. In their culture, they marry at a very young age, and once married, they cannot afford to leave their families in the village to attend Bible school in the city. I struggled to find a plan that would work. At one point, I tried Bible school seminars. When Missionary Evangelist Monte Showalter visited Belize, he introduced me to Bible School Extensions. This turned out to be the answer for Belize. The students met one day a week in a village near their own for Bible school classes.

With many extensions, I traveled a lot. I made all the books, then traveled to the villages to deliver them and to open classes each trimester. When we started the Bible school extensions, I graded all the homework and tests until I trained the teachers how to grade. Finding a suitable curriculum proved challenging since the students (primarily pastors) had only a third-grade education. While pastors had a knowledge of salvation and the Oneness doctrine, they lacked an overall knowledge of the Word. Exploring God's Word, the first class, proved to be the favorite class of most students.

As the pastors gained knowledge of the Word of God, they began sharing their increased knowledge in their churches. That, combined with the introduction of Sunday schools, resulted in students coming to Bible school with a basic knowledge of the Bible. In time, the Belize Bible School incorporated the GATS curriculum. Before I left Belize in 2018, Belize had six extensions and over forty graduates, with classes in three languages.

Along with Bible school, I assisted my dad in developing the national work. We formed a new constitution appropriate for Belize, which I translated into Spanish. The new constitution instituted ministerial credentials for the existing ministers and requirements for new ministers. The Mayan brethren were afraid of naming new leaders because they felt like they were not being loyal to the long-time leader. In time, the new constitution, an expanded organizational structure, and matured leadership resulted in explosive national church growth.

There had been no resident missionary in Belize for many years before my parents and I arrived in 1998. As a result, the pastors had received very little training. We began conducting training seminars. In the beginning, I served mainly as the interpreter. Throughout the years, we continued these training seminars. When growth allowed us to separate into single-language seminars, I also began teaching at the seminars.

We always dealt with translations because we had churches in four different languages. One time I translated during a wedding. The bride and the minister spoke Kekchi. The groom and I spoke Spanish. The minister and I spoke English. The minister asked the bride's vows in Kekchi and she responded. Then he translated them to me in English. In turn, I translated them into Spanish for the groom. For the groom's vows, the minister asked them in English, and I then translated them into Spanish for the groom, who then responded. I translated his response into English for the minister, who then translated them into Kekchi for the bride. I'll admit I got confused a time or two!

Belize Appointment

In 2002, after nearly thirteen years on AIM, I was appointed as an intermediate missionary at the General Conference in Phoenix, Arizona. I was ordained at a special service at World Evangelism Center in 2004. At the time of my 2002 appointment, my parents were on deputation, so I returned to Belize for about eighteen months before I began my first deputation.

In the meantime, I did all the legal work necessary to get the UPCIB registered with the government of Belize. Because Belize is a Commonwealth nation, I also took on the responsibility of getting all of our buildings approved as locations for weddings. I ensured that all of our ordained ministers were appointed marriage officers by the government.

During this time, I once again served as pastor of the English church and spoke weekly at the Spanish church. I also founded the National Sunday School Department and the National Ladies Ministries Department during these years. I conducted and taught children's ministry seminars and held children's crusades. Eventually, we started holding ladies conferences.

For eighteen years, I served as the national secretary. I represented Belize at the Global Council in Panama and again in Sri Lanka. For many years, I participated in the CAC RELCO (Central America/Caribbean Regional Leadership Conference) meetings representing Belize. Also, I was privileged to represent Belize at the Spanish Summit in the Dominican Republic and again in Guatemala.

Kenya and Vanuatu

In 2018, I felt my world was turning upside down when my time came to leave Belize. As I prayed and sought the will of God for my life, the Africa regional director, Randy Adams, asked me to go to Africa for three months to teach in a Bible school. When I asked which country in Africa, I was pleasantly surprised that he mentioned Kenya. As a child who had read all those books by missionaries, I had always wanted to go to Kenya.

As much as I enjoyed my time in Kenya and was honored to teach in the Bible school and speak at the national convention, I did not feel I was called to be there for the long term. As Bishop Karuku preached one Sunday morning, I talked to the Lord, asking Him what I was doing in Kenya and whether He had forgotten about me. At that moment, I felt the sweet presence of the Holy Ghost come over me, and I heard Him whisper into my spirit, "I haven't forgotten about you at all, Amy. No, Kenya is not My will for your future, but haven't you always wanted to come to Kenya? I brought you to Kenya just because I love you!" I was overwhelmed with emotion and began to cry. What an amazing and awesome God who *loves me!* Not only did He let me visit Kenya, but He allowed me to be used in the ministry in Kenya.

After Kenya, I went to the South Pacific Island of Vanuatu. I taught in the Bible school and served with the Preachers' Kid ministry there. I remained in Vanuatu for about a year and a half until I resigned due to health issues.

13

Guatemala

Lynne Jewett

Lynne Jewett (1989–Active)

Lynne Jewett first visited Guatemala in 1986. She had no plans to live on the mission field; her only intention was to visit Brad Thompson, who had been like a brother to her, and to check on him. When she arrived with their friends Peter Wright and Allen Lawson, she only intended to stay for three weeks before returning to her career as a medical technologist.

Her first trip to that mission field was not without incident. Guatemala was involved in a civil war during that time, and the group drove through gunfire more than once to reach their intended location. During one memorable service, a roach flew into Lynne's mouth mid-song. That was not her last roach encounter on that trip. On another occasion, she pulled back the covers of her bed to find it swarming with roaches. Although she slept through long nights clutching a can of bug repellant, she continued to fall in love with both the bug-infested country and its people.

Upon her return to Canada, she tried to convince herself that she was excited about what she had felt, seen, and heard only because she had never been on a missions trip before. Excitement wasn't the only long-lasting side effect of her trip, however. She had recognized things she could do to make a difference. She had seen how Wynn Drost had to stand in line at the bank for three hours. She had seen him operating the old Gestetner printer, the old-fashioned kind that involved putting ink in the drum and winding it up. They were working with the original "photocopy" machine, something like a duplicator. It was a simple task, but it took much of his time. She began to feel God calling her to be an extra pair of hands.

Back home, Lynne applied herself at her job for a year and then used her vacation time to travel to Europe to visit friends who were there on the AIM program. She returned from Europe still burdened for Guatemala.

In 1988, she revisited Guatemala, taking three girlfriends with her. When her friends got off the plane, they immediately uttered negative impressions like "It stinks here," "It's dirty," and "It doesn't look anything like the glory you described to us." But Lynne? She was in love. Her thoughts and feelings could not have been more contradictory to her friends' opinions. Guatemala was amazing! It was perfect! She was thrilled!

By November 1988, Lynne knew what she would do with her life and where she would live it. She would soon return to Guatemala where she belonged. Lynne's first official long-term missions trip to Guatemala was in 1989 as an AIMer under the supervision of Missionary T. W. Drost. Later, in 1992, she followed the Drost family to Mexico, where she worked in the national office, Bible school, and children's ministries for seven years. She learned invaluable lessons about organization, church work, and ministering to people. She also witnessed the supernatural provision of the Lord time and time again.

After seven years, Lynne returned to her "first love," Guatemala, where she became a fully appointed missionary in 1996. She has worked in Bible schools and children's ministries ever since.

Her burden for children has always been an indispensable part of her ministry. She feels that their strong faith and sincere understanding of the Word of God can be a limitless resource for the Kingdom. In 2002, she was appointed children's ministries coordinator for the Central America and Caribbean Region. She has traveled to many nations promoting children's ministries, teaching seminars, and holding children's crusades. Her goal has been to see Sunday school programs established in every Pentecostal church in her region.

In 2003, Lynne received her career missionary appointment after serving for fourteen years. For most of those years, she has had the privilege of working side-by-side with Brad and Regina Thompson, whom she considers great missionaries and true friends. She has served as a Bible school administrator for nearly twenty years, with over five hundred Bible school students each year and twenty-four schools in operation around the country.

Lynne began a new adventure in May 2011 by establishing the nonprofit association H.O.M.E. International (A Home for Orphans, Ministry, and Education). Land was purchased, and construction began in 2012. The administrators received their first child in October 2016. H.O.M.E. operates as a fully accredited children's home working with Child Protective Services for the abused and abandoned children of Guatemala.

At the beginning of the dream for this project, Lynne was told she would need at least one million dollars to get the operation up and running. The Lord bargained with her that He would take care of the rest if she would agree not to worry. At the time of this writing, the buildings are built, children have been rescued, and H.O.M.E. is fully functional.

Since the start of the project, God has called His people to invest over two million dollars into it. As a result of the UPCI Men's Ministry (Apostolic Man) and Global Missions working together, over three hundred men from thirty-one states and provinces have traveled to Guatemala to work on the project. They came from all over North America, stayed in hotels, paid for their own food, purchased building supplies, and built ten homes. They sacrificed to make a dream become a reality. The H.O.M.E. complex now includes an administration building, a multipurpose building, a well house, an AIM house (accommodations for short-term workers called "The Ponderosa"), a maintenance building, and the homes (houses) for the children—fifteen buildings in all, as well as a beautiful playground. All this happened within four years. Lynne could never have come up with the needed amount of money or manpower. The Lord did it. Lynne kept her word not to worry, and God kept His word—He provided!

Throughout Lynne's ministry, God has provided. He has been a constant companion, a source of strength, and the One who held her hand. She has been through gunfire and robbery, high mountains, and low valleys, and loves to tell the stories He will keep writing with her life. She keeps her word not to worry, and He keeps His word to provide.[1]

"Lynne is now the administrator for the Institute of Pentecostal Ministries in Guatemala and serves as the national Sunday school director."[2] In her book *Disasters Minister*, Lynne, with the assistance of Melinda Poitras, shares remarkable true stories revealing the realities that accompany commitment to a calling.[3]

PART IV
SOUTH AMERICA

14

Brazil

Margaret Calhoun and Ivana Norris

Margaret Calhoun (1968–1976)

A God-ordered encounter with deputizing missionaries, Bennie and Theresa DeMerchant, changed the course of Margaret Calhoun's teaching career. Before encountering the DeMerchants, she had met Pastor Jack and JoAnn Yonts in Madison, Wisconsin, and learned about the Apostolic message. The impact of these two Pentecostal couples prepared Margaret's heart to hear God's call into missions.

Margaret's parents, who were not Pentecostal believers, would not have known that their baby girl, born on December 6, 1932, would someday move to another continent as a missionary teacher and influence the eternal destiny of countless people. Margaret earned a bachelor's degree in elementary education at Indiana University and a master's degree in psychology and education from Butler University. She furthered her education at the University of Wisconsin. While in Madison, Wisconsin, the Yontses introduced her to the Pentecostal message, which she wholeheartedly embraced. Her baptism in Jesus' name and infilling of the Spirit further enhanced her kind and thoughtful nature.

Margaret's brief meeting with Bennie and Theresa DeMerchant triggered her desire to visit them on the mission field in Brazil. In July 1968, Margaret and a friend flew to Manaus, Brazil, after which Margaret applied for a missionary appointment to Brazil. She was appointed an assistant missionary at the 1968 General Conference in Atlantic City, New Jersey. On arrival in Brazil in 1969, she quickly adjusted and spent many hours on the riverboat teaching God's Word. She worked alone during the DeMerchants' furlough in 1970. In a report to the Foreign Missions Division, she stated that sixteen had received the Holy Ghost in Manaus and thirteen in the interior.[1] In 1971, when the DeMerchants returned and began flying the Sheaves for Christ floatplane along the Amazon, she frequently visited the jungle churches.

When Margaret returned to the States for furlough in 1973, she served on the original committee that developed Overseas Ministries to provide training materials for missionaries to equip nationals for ministry. After raising her Partners in Missions support in record time, she worked at the World Evangelism Center writing training materials for Overseas Ministries. Her ministry lives on through the materials she wrote.

On her return to Brazil following deputation, she resumed traveling and teaching along the Amazon River. Her missionary years ended tragically on Tuesday, August 31, 1976. The accident and its aftermath are described in the book, *Full Throttle!* by Bennie DeMerchant and Dolly McElhaney.

> Sister Margaret, who had been teaching in the Bible school in Rio, was filling in the thirty-day time gap between the departure of the Mark Norris family from Rio de Janeiro, who had supervised the DeMerchants' work in Manaus for nearly a year but had to return to Rio before Bennie's . . . arrival. Sister Margaret wanted to get back to Rio and was scheduled to leave on the Monday after Bennie and

company arrived Saturday from Canada with the new airplane.

Early on the morning of the anticipated flight to Maués, someone clapped his hands at the door. It was Jose Cinque, a young single man who [had] graduated from the Bible school in Rio and had spent over a year in the beginnings of the distant church on the Juruá River in Eirunepé. A suitcase dangled from his right hand.

"Pastor Bennie," he said, "I would go with you to Maués."

"Jose, you just got a new job!" Bennie exclaimed. "You better stick with the new job lest the manager at the hotel dismiss you. There will be other opportunities [for you] to visit Maués."

"Oh, no, Pastor Bennie," Jose hurried to explain. "My manager is allowing me to go."

Bennie took Beth [the DeMerchants' daughter] aside. "Beth, would you stay here? After all, you've had enough floatplane flying from Canada to Brazil. Would you give your place to Jose?"

A crestfallen Beth reluctantly agreed, for she had eagerly anticipated being with Sister Margaret for the day.

So on Tuesday afternoon at about 2 o'clock, Bennie, Clayton [Bennie's longtime friend from Canada], Sister Margaret, and Jose buckled themselves inside the new plane for a visit to this area southeast of Manaus.

As they climbed into the plane, Sister Margaret stepped back a moment to admire it. "Brother Bennie," she said, "this plane is so huge and new, it should last for many years of good service."

Bennie water-taxied the Cessna 206 floatplane N-35502 at the mouth of Taraumã Creek toward Rio Negro Bay. But while Bennie and Clayton checked and readied the plane to go full throttle in this, the new plane's first missions flight, the sky darkened over the city eight miles to the east as a rain shower and its accompanying ground wind approached.

Beyond the trees on the point of land ahead and to the right lay a body of water fourteen miles long. The wind lashed its surface into six-foot waves, but where the plane floated in the sheltered cove, the water was only slightly choppy.

The plane lifted into the air. To avoid the squall, then about four miles away, Bennie circumnavigated it to the south and banked the plane in a right turn toward the bay at about one hundred feet of altitude. He was talking with the microphone to the control tower when without warning the engine abruptly stopped.

The plane was turned with its wings perpendicular to the big waves. At its low altitude, Bennie had no room to turn back straight into the wind. He was in a dreaded crosswind situation with no power. The little altitude he had was bleeding away fast! He hit the emergency fuel pump switch. The fuel pump snarled as the whine of the propeller diminished. As Bennie rounded out of the glide above the waves, the three-bladed propeller stopped completely. The pontoons squashed on the water parallel with the high waves.

This is definitely the wrong way to land a seaplane in a strong crosswind, Bennie thought. . . . Bennie used the ailerons to the maximum to hold down the left wing to balance the plane as much as possible. A mountainous black wave surged in from the left. He glanced at the right wing tip as it neared the water and knew what would happen when it struck. He grabbed the V bar in the windshield. He was helpless to control the effects of the wind as that wing struck the water.

No one spoke a word. Absolute silence filled the aircraft.

The water grabbed the wing and cartwheeled the plane. It landed upside down in the river. Immediately, water rushed in and completely flooded the cabin. The impact jammed the flaps of the wing against the two double doors on the right side of the plane where Sister Margaret and Jose were sitting.

Underwater, Bennie reached around and three different times grabbed the door handle and twisted it to force this door open. It would not budge. . . . Bennie swam quickly inside the water-filled cabin to the rear baggage area. Some floating suitcases blocked his view as he groped in vain for . . . a baggage-door latch on this new plane. Bennie was a strong swimmer and could hold his breath over a minute under water, but he realized that he was trapped inside the rear of this plane. In the murk, he spotted a little plastic, trapezoid-shaped window about his size.

He pounded it three or four times with his fist. The center part of it finally broke, leaving jagged pieces of plastic protruding from its edges. Ignoring damage to his fist, he struck the window several times until he was able to get his head and shoulders out. His shirt ripped as he struggled through. But the small opening held him fast around his belt line.

Bennie was trapped and by then taking in water. His mind raced. He could go no further and needed air. His whole past life and call to the Amazon flashed before him.

Jesus! Help me get clear of this wreckage under this river. I want to see many more churches come to existence in the Amazon! his heart cried. At that point, he kicked hard and felt his thighs and knees scrape through the window!

He was free. He reached the light on the surface and between high waves gulped in air and looked around. He saw only the bottoms of the pontoons of the submerged aircraft with its wing shadow underneath. As the banana-like pontoons dived into a wave and emerged on the other side, Bennie spotted the head of his front-seat passenger, Clayton Goodine, who had also somehow escaped.

Where were the heads of the other two? They could not be seen in the water.

A speedboat containing five or six men bounced on the waves and stopped beside the overturned aircraft. On the beach a few hundred feet away, they had witnessed it all.

"Two people are still in the plane!" Bennie yelled.

The men, already wearing swimming trunks, dived down each side of the plane and resurfaced several times.

"We can't get inside!" they yelled, and dived again and again.

Too weak to do much more than gulp air, a desperate Bennie urged the men on.

"We'll give these folks mouth-to-mouth resuscitation," he promised.

After half an hour, the men claimed it was useless to continue. They tied a rope from the boat to the submerged plane and towed it very slowly upside down toward shallower water. . . .

Over the next seventy-two hours, Bennie received visits from aeronautical officials and fielded national and international phone calls. He preached Jose's funeral. During the same time, he completed the paperwork for the release to ship Sister Margaret's remains to the United States for a funeral later preached in Indianapolis by Brother Nathaniel A. Urshan. . . .

The loss of two lives weighed heavily on Bennie. His head drooped low. Upon his shoulders rested the deaths of two young people who had been so instrumental in the work of God. Exhausted and knocked flat on his face, he thought, *If one day there ever will be a strong, widespread Pentecostal church in northern Brazil, it will be God's work and not mine. . . .*

At the end of September 1976, the whole fellowship sadly paid tribute to Sister Margaret at General Conference with thousands of ministers and members present. The news of the deaths of Sister Margaret in the United States and of Jose Cinque in Brazil stirred many of the young ministers to step into the work to fill their place wherever God called them, regardless of the sacrifice they might make one day.

> Over the ensuing years, busloads from 125 churches in the Manaus area have driven to that same beach where the accident happened to have church and baptize hundreds of believers, with a dozen ministers baptizing folks in Jesus' name in one setting. How great is our God![2]

Though Margaret Calhoun's missionary years ended abruptly in her second term, the seeds planted in her first term began producing an abundant harvest. During the four years following her death, the DeMerchants saw an astounding revival—over four thousand were baptized, eighty national pastors received ministerial licenses, and fifty-three churches were started.[3]

"A thousand miles from the mouth of the Amazon stands a church building filled with people who owe their salvation to this missionary lady."[4] A Margaret Calhoun Memorial Training and Convention Center was built in Rio de Janeiro, Brazil, to honor this tremendous missionary. Participants in the dedication included Missionary Field Superintendent Robert Norris, Philip Walmer, and Mark Norris.[5]

Though Margaret's missionary years (1968–1976) spanned only eight years (one term and a partial term), her ministry continues in the lives of Apostolic Brazilians. At the time of this writing, forty-seven years have passed, but the Word endures! During her forty-three years and eight months on earth (December 6, 1932–August 31, 1976), Margaret planted seeds of truth; others have watered, and the harvest continues to increase.

Ivana Norris (Single 2015–Active)

Born into a Roman Catholic family in the state of Bahia, Brazil, Ivana knew nothing about the Pentecostal experience. Missionary Robert Norris introduced her family to the Apostolic message, and Ivana became the fruit of a missionary's ministry. Ivana studied at the Bible school in Rio, was baptized in Jesus' name, and received the baptism of the Holy Ghost. After three years, she moved to Rio de Janeiro, where she earned a degree as a bilingual translator. Recognizing her qualifications, Robert Norris asked her to teach in the Bible school.

In God's time, Ivana married the Norrises' son, Jeffrey. As a couple, Jeffrey and Ivana Norris were appointed to Brazil in 1987. They served together for twenty-eight years until Jeffrey's death in 2015. After his death, Ivana continued on the field. She directs the Bible school, where she also teaches. This was the first Bible school founded in Brazil by Robert Norris in 1971. In addition, she teaches, preaches, and translates in seminars in different states of Brazil. Many ministers from all over Brazil have graduated from this Bible school. As a missionary, she has served as the National Ladies leader, Rio District vice-president, and Rio District Ladies leader for over twenty-eight years. She also serves as Rio District secretary and National Prayer leader.

Ivana has been pastoring a church for fifteen years in Costa Barros, one of the most dangerous slums in Rio. God has protected her and given her favor. Many souls have been saved and changed, even those of drug dealers. She desires to do more for the kingdom of God as she continues her teaching and pastoral ministries.

Through Ivana's faithful labor, the ministry of Robert and Jeanne Norris continues. In answering the call to

Brazil, the Norrises could not have predicted future significant happenings. First, their son Jeffrey married Ivana, a Brazilian lady, who had accepted the Apostolic message under the Norris family ministry. Then Jeffrey and Ivana served as appointed missionaries to Brazil for over two decades. Significantly, after the deaths of Jeffrey and his parents, Ivana continues to plant truth and reap an Apostolic harvest in Brazil.

15

Ecuador

Lucile Farmer

Lucile Farmer, Ecuador (Appointment 1963–August 1969) (Israel 1971–1979)

At age forty-eight, twenty-one years after she first heard the voice of the Lord calling her to missionary work, Lucile Farmer, according to her words, "stood on the steps of a little country store in the jungles of western Ecuador, the sights and sounds around me new to this novice missionary." Standing on the steps of the country store, she began reflecting on her call and the long road to its fulfillment. Highlights of her story have been recorded in the book *A Willing Heart.*[1]

Lucile's call to missions had come while she stood washing dishes after assisting with the birth of a friend's baby. Just months before, her husband had deserted her and left her alone to care for four children ranging in age from six months to five years. She kept the calling a precious secret for a time, accepting that she must first raise her children. Finally, at age forty-eight, she stood on foreign soil in Ecuador, reflecting on the long road she had traveled.

Lucile grew up during the Great Depression in a home with a physically abusive father who forbade the family to attend a Pentecostal church. Two Pentecostal neighbors dared to visit them and bring them the church news. School and occasional picnics became Lucile's only outlets for escaping the terrible troubles at home. When Lucile turned nineteen, a young man began visiting her.

This angered her father. However, after several visits and a proposal, her father consented to their marriage. While Lucile was grateful for a respite from the troubled, fear-filled years, married life with the birth of four children within six years brought its burdens. Discouragement, sparse finances, and frequent moves with her husband's job changes forced Lucile to move back to her parents' home several times.

A brighter day came for Lucile when Elmo, her brother, decided to move from the family home and make a place for Lucile and her children. After fourteen years without attending church, Lucile and her brother returned to church. Lucile's husband continued to come and go on jobs, moving the family from place to place. He moved out when Lucile was pregnant with their fourth child, and his promised financial help never came. Lucile didn't see him again for twelve years. While raising her children, Lucile served in home missions churches in Wyoming and Mexico and pastored in Washington.

While serving as a pastor in Montesano, Washington, she felt the day had come for her to answer God's call to Ecuador. She wrote to Missions Director Wynn Stairs expressing her desire. He responded that the missions board no longer appointed single women as missionaries, causing Lucile, with encouragement from others, to make plans to go to Ecuador on her own. However, on the advice of her district superintendent, she attended the UPC General Conference in October 1963, where she met the missionary board and received an appointment to Ecuador twenty-one years after hearing God's call.

After being appointed, Lucile traveled for a few weeks in California and the Northwest. She visited her children while awaiting word from the UPC Foreign Missions

Division about her departure for Ecuador. On the way to the field in April 1964, she stopped in Colombia and spent nearly two months with Missionary Sallie Morley to practice her Spanish. Thirty years earlier, Lucile had studied Spanish, but she knew she needed to review her grammar and vocabulary. While in Colombia, she also traveled alone up into the mountains (as Sallie suggested) to visit some churches and experience traveling solo.

The early-morning prayer meetings of the Colombian church impressed Lucile. By the time the pastor opened the church about a quarter before five, some people had already arrived, not owning a clock to know the exact time. Some often stayed to pray until about seven o'clock. Lucile felt convinced that the morning prayer meetings accounted for Colombia's continuous spirit of revival.

Lucile arrived in Ecuador on June 5, 1964, with no one to meet her since she had to fly a day earlier than initially scheduled. She hired a taxi to take her to Pastor Limones's address. When she arrived at the Limones home, she was welcomed by the Limoneses and by Argemira, a lady in her twenties. Back in 1959 during a visit with the Morleys in Colombia, Lucile had met these Colombians. Later, the Limoneses and Argemira had moved to Ecuador, where they established seven churches. As it turned out, Argemira arrived at the Limones home in Quito the same day Lucile arrived, ready to travel and visit the churches. Thus, Lucile began her missionary work the next day. On this first travel day, she met one of the most important contacts of her time in Ecuador.

The account of Lucile's travel on her second day in Ecuador, plus some other selected excerpts from her book, *A Willing Heart,* provide glimpses of the uncertainties, challenges, and difficulties of missionary life as faced by early UPC missionaries.

During her first church service in Ecuador (at the Santo Domingo church, a several-hour bus trip from Quito), Lucile met Lino, who had begun attending the Santo Domingo church, a three-hour bus trip from his home. Unknown to Lucile, Lino would become an essential part of the work in Ecuador. He desired to be baptized and receive the Holy Spirit, but he faced a problem. Though he lived with a woman and they had twin daughters, they were not married, a common situation among the poor people in Ecuador. He was interested in the "new religion" preached by the Colombians, but his partner showed no interest. Lino invited Lucile and Argemira to stop by his house on their way from Santo Domingo to visit the church in Esmeraldas, a small town on the coast. They agreed to his request.

As they arrived at Lino's home, his neighbors began drifting in until about thirty-five people filled his small house. The people's interest inspired Lino to plead with Lucile and Argemira to return weekly. However, the distance by bus to his home was six hours for Lucile and seven hours for Argemira. When the ladies reached Esmeraldas, they discussed Lino's request with the pastor. The three agreed to share the responsibility of holding services in Lino's home. Thus, Lucile's first church in Ecuador officially opened.

Lucile planned to return the following Sunday. Unfortunately, a thief stole her purse that week as she boarded a city bus in Quito. She lost her Ecuadorian money, American dollars, and temporary visa. She had just withdrawn money from the bank for the trip to Lino's house. She could not travel without a visa and had to remain in Quito until she received a permanent visa. Three weeks passed before she and Argemira could visit the new church in Lino's home. When they arrived, they found a changed man—sad in expression but radiant in spirit.

During the three weeks Lucile could not travel, meetings had continued in Lino's home. Then his family abruptly walked out—his "woman" with the twins, his father, his brother, and his cousin. Left alone, he traveled to Santo Domingo, where the pastor (a Colombian) baptized him. The next day, a Sunday, he received the Holy Spirit. Lucile and Argemira arrived two days later and found a transformed young man. That night, they had a good service in his home.

The ladies returned the following week and found that Lino had moved a Colombian family from the Santo Domingo church into his home to live with him and work for him. On a leased plot of land, he raised bananas for export to the United States. The Colombian family, with their four daughters (ages five to twelve) and toddler son, were a great asset to the young church. Even the young girls could lead the church in singing hymns and choruses.

On her bus trip to Lino's place a few weeks later, Lucile was joined by thirty-five other Pentecostals returning home after fifteen of the group had been baptized in Santo Domingo. When she got off the bus, they decided to join her to have service that night with Lucile preaching. Lucile tried to excuse herself from speaking to the group with her limited Spanish, but Lino insisted. She handled "one-on-one" conversations reasonably well, but speaking to a larger group seemed beyond her ability.

As Lucile spoke that evening, she could hear through the thin walls the prayers and sobs of a mother caring for her dying child. The following morning, she helped the grieving mother wash and dress the baby for burial. Later that day, they walked seven kilometers to the nearest cemetery to bury the baby. Thus, Lucile's missionary years began with long bus rides, initial contacts, conversions, and sorrows.

The church, which was started near Lino's home, soon grew, with people being baptized and Spirit-filled. However, after six months, the pastor helping with the church was transferred away. At this time, Lino, a six-month-old believer, began preaching to fill the gap, and the church continued to grow. When he came into the church, he could neither read nor write. Lucile wrote, "He felt a great desire to be able to read the Bible, so he began to fast and pray. The Lord Himself taught Brother Lino how to read."[2] As he grew in the Lord, he began traveling and preaching on banana plantations. By the time Lucile left Ecuador five years later, Lino was supervising twelve churches he had helped to establish.

Lino prayed for one and a half years for his "woman" to give her heart to God. While she occasionally attended services, she never became a Christian. Eventually, she began living with Lino's cousin and had a child with him. Lino then started praying for a godly wife, and God provided him with a Spirit-filled woman who converted to truth just before she was scheduled to take her permanent vows to become a nun. At his request, Lucile helped him select the trousseau for his bride since it was customary for the man to buy the wedding dress and trousseau. Lino's story illustrates how a missionary's first contact can be the foundation for planting truth in new areas.

Lucile's living situation differed considerably from that of later missionaries. When she first arrived in Quito, she lived with a couple from the Quito church as arranged by

Pastor Limones. The couple lived in two rooms with three children (two young boys and a baby girl). With the help of Lucile's rent, they moved into a small three-bedroom apartment. After some time, Lucile moved to Quinindé in western central Ecuador. At the invitation of Lino and his new wife, she lived with them for the first two months of their marriage. Lino wanted Lucile to teach his wife about being a pastor's wife. Lucile wrote that life in the jungle was not easy. She had little fresh meat and no fresh milk, but she desired to live in Quinindé to share the gospel.

Lucile wrote that she felt strongly impressed to make a trip to Quito one day. When she went to the post office the morning after reaching Quito, she found a telegram from Oscar Vouga, UPC Foreign Missions director. The telegram informed her that he was arriving at the airport that day. She hurriedly took a taxi to the airport to meet him. During his visit of a few days, he informed her that she must return to live in Quito. He told her, "This is the capital, so we must establish a strong work here in Quito before branching out into other places. I want you to work here until this work grows; then we can think about going into other places."[3]

Lucile wrote that she witnessed many healings and miracles in Ecuador. On one occasion, a believer asked Lucile to visit a sick lady who had been unable to get out of bed for four years and could not care for her four children when her husband was away. Her children did the work as she supervised them from her bed. The family lived in one room with a crude lean-to kitchen, and they cooked over an open fire.

When Lucile entered the room, she remembered a pastor telling her to check for images or holy pictures before praying. If there were such items, he would ask for the person to give them to him to be destroyed before he would pray. Remembering this, Lucile entered the humble room (with two ladies accompanying her), read some Scripture verses, and made a few comments. Then she asked, "Would you like us to pray for you?"[4]

When the lady said, "Yes, I would," Lucile asked about the pictures on the wall and a statue of Mary. Then Lucile explained that she could not pray unless the lady gave up these things. To Lucile's surprise, the sick lady agreed. Lucile prayed a simple prayer for the lady's healing, and the three ladies left to make other visits that day.

The ladies left the one-room home and climbed about one hundred steps to the street. As they stood at the top of the stairs discussing where to go next, Lucile turned and spotted the woman they had just prayed for climbing up the steps. The Lord had miraculously healed her. The lady and her four children attended the open-air campaign every night in the following days.

The lady suffered persecution from her husband for attending the Pentecostal church. Lucile advised her to be patient with him and pray for his conversion. In time, the husband ordered her out of the house with the children. She came to Lucile asking if she could leave the children with her while she looked for a place to live. With the pastor's approval, Lucile curtained off a portion of her big room to provide a place for the lady and her children. The lady kept the house clean and did all of the cooking in Lucile's home. She did housekeeping jobs whenever possible to provide for her children. The family stayed with Lucile for five months until Lucile moved away from the city.[5]

Lucile wrote that open-air campaigns were one tool for reaching Ecuador's people. Pastor Limones in Quito loved to evangelize and hold revivals. Meetings would be held for two months, with one to two hundred people attending nightly. One night, Lucile heard a noise that she couldn't identify. She described it as the "roar of an angry bull." Suddenly, a large group of young people emerged from behind the buildings and swept down the hill, making an angry sound. It was later learned that they had destroyed a recreation hall built by a club from the United States. Thankfully, they did not disrupt the meeting.

On another night, the mounted police came and warned the crowd, "Get out of here quick! There's a mob coming!" They dispersed, and the large rocks thrown into the meeting place injured no one. Communist agitation and nationalist feelings affected the churches in both Colombia and Ecuador at that time.

In August 1968, after returning from a visit to some of the churches, Lucile began to think about her upcoming furlough in 1969. Thoughts about seeing her family members in the States created a feeling of homesickness, which she had seldom experienced. Then her thoughts wandered to what she would do on her return to Ecuador. She envisioned having a little camper trailer and traveling to the various churches. The camper would provide privacy and conveniences she had seldom enjoyed during her first term in Ecuador. As she thought about these plans, the Lord spoke very clearly to her: "You won't be coming back to Ecuador." This shocked her. She had gone to Ecuador with the idea that she would spend the rest of her life there.[6]

After praying about this for a while, Lucile wrote to Missions Director Oscar Vouga, telling him to send a replacement as she would not be returning to Ecuador. Earlier, she had asked him to consider sending a man to head the work. Interestingly, around the time she informed Director Vouga to look for a replacement, God had been dealing with Pastor Daniel Scott in West Virginia about Ecuador. As it turned out, the Scotts applied and received an appointment to Ecuador, arriving in April 1969. Their arrival on the field turned out much like Lucile's. They came by taxi with their three children to her address before their telegram reached her. She welcomed the children by giving them a cute puppy with a red ribbon tied around its neck.

Providentially, God sent two missionary couples to replace Lucile. Missionaries to Uruguay, Elga and Claree Battle, came through Ecuador on their way home for furlough. At that time, they planned to request an appointment to Venezuela. After they met the Ecuadorian pastors, Lucile secretly hoped they would feel directed to Ecuador. When they and the Scotts received appointments to Ecuador, Lucile felt that her prayers for a man to lead the work in Ecuador were answered.

Before Lucile left Ecuador, the Scotts persuaded her to apply for reappointment as they felt they needed her help. Against her better judgment, she applied and was appointed. However, four months after her arrival in Ecuador, Lucille received an express letter informing her that her mother was not expected to live. She hurriedly returned to the States to care for her mother until her passing in December 1969. The following year, Lucile lived with family members and worked different jobs until receiving an invitation to work as the cook for Harvest Homes in Portland, Oregon. Although she knew that her time in Ecuador was over, missionary work remained in her heart. A dream she had had before leaving Ecuador—a dream of very dry, round hills with a terraced look—began to direct her thoughts.[7]

Lucile's Missionary Years in Israel without an Appointment (1971–1978)

While reading her Bible in Ecuador after having the dream, Lucile had felt the dream related to the hills of Israel. Back in the States in February 1970, she saw a picture of Golda Meir and began to feel great compassion for her and the country of Israel. Feeling burdened for Israel, she prayed much for the country and began reading old *National Geographic* magazines about Israel and the surrounding countries.

In June 1970, as Lucile washed pots and pans in the Harvest Homes kitchen, Missionary Director T. F. Tenney came to see her. He said, "This is no job for a missionary."

She replied, "Well, it is a job."

Lucile followed his advice and met the missionary board during the August General Conference in Portland, Oregon. When a board member asked if she had thought about going to some other country as a missionary, she replied. "It's in my heart to go to Israel." When the board told her that Israel was closed to missionaries, she expressed interest in going wherever she might be needed. However, nothing was decided regarding a possible appointment at that conference.[8] Lucile began fasting and praying for the Lord's direction.

God's direction came to Lucile one night in a vision as she knelt praying at the Portland church she attended. She felt the powerful presence of Jesus as He spoke to her: "Now is the time to go." As she continued praying much about the matter, she began planning to go on her own. She wrote to Director Tenney and informed him of her decision.[9]

Learning of a young man with a Bible center on the Mount of Olives, Lucile wrote to him asking about the cost of living in Jerusalem. He informed her that the costs would be about the same as in the US. Not knowing exactly where to go in Israel, she wrote to a lady whose family had established an American group that ran a hospital in the Old City, information she had found in a *National Geographic* magazine. Lucile offered to work in the hospital as a volunteer in return for room and board. Two months passed before Lucile received an answer from the lady's daughter with news that her mother had passed away. However, the daughter had taken Lucile's letter to a girls' orphanage north of Jerusalem.[10]

As it turned out, Lucile received a letter from the girls' orphanage inviting her to serve as a volunteer cook for the teachers and house mothers. She accepted their offer and prepared to leave without delay. Even before receiving the letter, she had given her notice to Harvest Homes that she would be leaving at the end of February. In the weeks before Lucile left for Israel, she had two dreams that assured her of God's direction. She visited a few churches and her children before flying to Miami. While with friends in Miami, she called the airlines and asked, "How soon can I make reservations to go to Israel?"

"Today if you want," came the reply.

"Not today," she told them, "but I'd like to go tomorrow."[11]

Thus, Lucile took her flight from America, though somewhat anxious about the unknowns, knowing that God had directed her decision to go to Israel. She arrived in Tel Aviv, Israel, on April 14, 1971. Personnel from the girls' home met her, taking her to her new home in the darkness of night. When she looked out the third-floor window the next morning, she saw the brown, terraced hills she had dreamed about three years earlier.[12] As she cooked at the girls' home, she continued fasting and praying, knowing God had other plans for her in Israel.

She contacted Shlomo Hizak, a young Jew who had a Bible center, to inform him that she was in the country. Not hearing from him, she took a bus, hoping to find the Bible center. Not finding it, she asked an Arab who sold donkey rides if he knew Shlomo Hizak. He did, calling him the Hallelujah Man. He insisted that she ride his donkey to the Bible center. Shlomo happily greeted Lucile and invited her to attend an Arabic Pentecostal conference that day. There she met the young Arab pastor leading the conference, who invited her to address the conference that afternoon. He introduced her to his blind aunt, Hilweh Karraha, who interpreted for her. Hilweh had been baptized in Jesus' name by Timothy Urshan and had received the Holy Ghost when she was about twenty years old. Lucile and Hilweh's friendship continued through the years.[13]

After attending the Jerusalem conference, Lucile returned to her cooking job but continued praying about her future. In one of the morning staff meetings, Lucile gave a Bible study on the baptism of the Holy Spirit. Only one other lady was Spirit-filled. Lucile and this lady prayed daily for the ninety-five girls, who seemed indifferent to spiritual matters. However, more than a year later, an Arab evangelist ministered at the school, resulting in the principal and forty-five girls receiving the Holy Spirit.

Before Lucile left the school, she had one more opportunity to bring a Bible study. This time she taught about baptism in the name of Jesus. When she finished teaching, the school supervisor jumped to his feet and said, "This is what Brother John brought to us when we formed our sisterhood." Lucile learned that John (Jan) was a Spirit-filled young Dutchman who was the warden of the Garden Tomb.[14]

About two weeks before Lucile's planned departure from the girls' school, she received a troubling call from Hilweh. The home for the Blind was closing, and the personnel wanted to send her to another home in the north. She felt distressed about leaving the forty to fifty children, mainly from Muslim homes, whom she was teaching in a rented apartment. When Lucile saw the children, she decided she wanted to join Hilweh in teaching them. So both of them moved into the apartment at a cost of thirty dollars per month. Unfortunately, a short time later, the owner gave notice that he needed the apartment for his son, who was getting married. After much searching, they found another apartment, but the rent was ninety-six dollars a month. Lucile agreed to pay half the rent as the Lord supplied.[15] And the Lord did supply!

Around the time that Lucile felt directed to leave her cooking job, her brother, David Darrah, visited Israel with a group of ministers. She traveled with them for five days, enjoying the fellowship. She paid her initial share of the rent from an impromptu offering they gave her before they departed. Some of the pastors in that group became her principal source of support during the remainder of her years in Israel, with George Thompson's church sending the majority of her support.[16]

Lucile visited the Bible center operated by Shlomo Hizak two or three times after first meeting him. Each time he invited her to help them at the center. After some time, Lucile accepted his offer, feeling somewhat discontent with doing much housework and having limited time for visitation while living with Hilweh. After arranging for an old friend of Hilweh to move in with her, Lucile moved to Jerusalem where she lived in a house not far from the Bible center. After the move, she began taking night classes in Hebrew.

While working at the Bible center, Lucile's witness resulted in Shlomo's secretary deciding to be baptized. When Lucile told her she would arrange for one of the visiting ministers to baptize her, the lady requested that Lucile baptize her. Thus, Lucile and a visiting friend from Arkansas took the lady with them to the Sea of Galilee, and Lucile baptized her where the Jordan River flows from the Sea of Galilee.[17]

During her years in Israel, Lucile met and interacted with others who came to minister there. In the early 1970s, Lucile met three Arabs (Costa Deir, Fahed Karmout, and John Kershaw) who had received the Holy Spirit in special meetings in Israel in 1947. Israel had received its statehood shortly after these men received the Spirit, and the three moved. Fahed Karmout moved to Jerusalem, began attending a Baptist church (no Pentecostal churches existed there yet), and eventually became the pastor. He pastored for many years, hiding his knowledge of Jesus Name baptism and the infilling of the Holy Spirit. Costa Deir, who had a Greek father and an Arab mother, went to the United States and became a national evangelist. In 1971, he returned to Israel to visit his friend, Fahed Karmout. He preached in the Baptist church in Jerusalem and other Baptist churches. His ministry resulted in Fahed's wife receiving the Holy Spirit. When this happened, Fahed baptized her and their children in Jesus' name. In time, hundreds of Arabs in Israel received baptism in Jesus' name.

After preaching in several Roman Catholic and Baptist churches, Costa Deir held a conference for missionaries from Anglican, Baptist, Lutheran, and other faiths, which Lucile attended. Costa preached about the baptism of the Holy Spirit. When the meeting ended that afternoon, Costa planned to go with a Baptist pastor to Nazareth. Before they left, the pastor asked, "How can I receive the baptism of the Holy Spirit?" As soon as Costa finished explaining, the pastor raised his hands and began speaking in other tongues. Lucile shared that a great outpouring of the Spirit spread across the land over the next two years, and many of those filled were missionaries from various churches.[18]

A few months after Costa Deir's visit, Lucile wrote John Kershaw and his wife about these events, and John, by that time living in the United States, came to visit his old friend, Fahed Karmout. The two had not seen each other for about twenty-five years. While John was in Israel, he witnessed to a young Spirit-filled Arab from Jordan about baptism in Jesus' name. Later, in the United States, this man was baptized. He traveled to many places, especially in Israel, baptizing people in the name of Jesus.[19] One of the places where he preached was at the girls' school where Lucile had first worked. His ministry there resulted in the school's principal and over half of the ninety-five girls receiving the Holy Spirit, an answer to Lucile's prayers.[20]

When Lucile finished her Hebrew studies, she volunteered at a Bible shop between Old and New Jerusalem, where she had many interesting conversations about the Bible. While serving there, she realized she needed to renew her visa, and a young man offered to help her. In the process he learned that the Interior Department had a thick file on Lucile documenting everywhere she went and everything she did. He was told that she would have to leave the Bible shop to get her visa renewed. During this period, civil disturbances and the detonation of bombs were common. In 1975, Tom Marshall and family (appointed UPCI missionaries) arrived to observe conditions before moving to Israel.[21] Before the arrival of the Tom Marshalls in August 1976, Lucile found an apartment for them and helped paint it.

Lucile's missionary years in Israel spanned about seven years, during which she witnessed many miracles and conversions to the Apostolic faith. Along with telling about spiritual victories, Lucile related in her book about receiving the shocking news of her daughter's death by suicide. Lucile's concern for souls was seen in the conversion of Greg and Beverly Wooten, an American couple who had moved to Israel. Through her influence and the ministry of the Marshalls, the Wootens—whose ministry later became known among Apostolics—studied God's Word and received the Apostolic experience.[22] As it turned out, Lucile moved from Jerusalem to work with the Wootens in Elias for a season.

In 1978, Lucile received an unexpected blow—a letter from Israel's Interior Department notifying her they had canceled her visa. Though shocked, she considered this as possibly God's answer to her children's insistence that she return home due to health issues related to Lucile's recent Parkinson's diagnosis. When she decided it was God's will for her to return home, no reservations were available for some time. However, exceptional provisions began unfolding.[23]

As it turned out, a young man named Danny assisted Lucile in buying a lower-priced tourist ticket without a long wait. When she checked in for her flight, the agent accepted her two oversized and overweight bags without additional charges. On the layover in Copenhagen as she waited to board the bus to the airport, a dignified doorman called her name and escorted her to a taxi for transport to the airport. At the airport the taxi driver picked up her bags and marched her to the check-in counter, bypassing the line. The ticket agent invited her to check her carry-on without cost, even though she had two checked bags. When she arrived in Seattle and walked down the ramp, a lady met her, saying, "I'm a service representative. I've come to help you through customs." Lucile wrote that she had dreaded clearing through customs. As it turned out, the lady located Lucile's bags and assisted her in checking in for her final flight to Portland. The lady seated Lucile in the boarding area for her three-hour wait to board, saying, "I'll be sitting right over here. If you have any other problems, just come and let me know."[24]

After arriving home, Lucile wrote a letter to Danny, who had assisted her in obtaining her ticket. After some weeks, the letter came back stamped "Person Unknown." This puzzled Lucile before her son Hugh responded, "Mom, don't you see? Danny was an angel."

In reading the account of her trip home from Israel, a reader would likely concur with her son Hugh that angels had assisted her. Lucile wrote, "It would be just like God to do something special for a weary soldier heading home."[25]

Further details of Lucile's productive and sacrificial five years of ministry as a pioneer missionary in Ecuador can be read in *Profiles of Pentecostal Missionaries* and *A Willing Heart*. When health issues brought Lucile back to the States, she helped Pastor Ray and Becky Sirstad establish a home missions work in Hood River, Oregon. Disabled with Parkinson's disease in her final years, she still faithfully attended church services and early morning prayer meetings. After moving into a care facility, she still came to church, even though she had to be lifted in and out of the car. Her mind remained sharp, and she sometimes added comments to teachings on the Word of God. On December 20, 1997, at age eighty-one (eleven days before her eighty-second birthday), Lucile entered her eternal home.

16

Colombia

Pearl Cooper, Bernice Davis, Barbara Flannery, Sallie Lemons (Morley)

Pearl Cooper (1948)

Pearl Cooper's name appears on the 1948 list of UPC missionaries "on the field" in Colombia, as noted in the June 1948 *Pentecostal Herald.*[1]

Bernice Davis (1946–1948)

The Evolving World of Foreign Missions lists Bernice Davis as one of the "missionaries recommended by the FMD and appointed by the General Presbyters at the 1946 General Conference." Her appointment was to South America, with no specific country identified.[2] She was listed as "outgoing" to South America in the June 1948 *Pentecostal Herald.*[3] Before her appointment, Bernice had attended the Pentecostal Bible Institute in Tupelo, Mississippi.

Barbara Flannery (1973–1986) — Colombia to Ecuador and back to Colombia

Barbara was a public-school teacher before becoming a home missionary in Alaska and later a missionary assistant in South America. Barbara received her UPCI appointment as an assistant missionary to Colombia at the 1973 General Conference.[4] She arrived in Colombia in 1974 and worked there until 1976, when she moved to Quito, Ecuador, to teach in the Bible school. In 1982, she returned to Colombia to work in the Bible school there.

Her steady resourcefulness served as a positive influence on the students.

By 1984 she was nearing the end of her second term on the field.[5] In the *Foreign Missions Story–1986*, Barbara described her work as a training ministry for ladies, Sunday school workers, youth leaders, and pastors. She helped establish Bible schools in both Ecuador and Colombia.[6] She worked with Missionaries Sidney and Mary Perdue in both Colombia and Ecuador. Barbara resigned from her missionary post in 1986.

Sallie Lemons (Morley) (1948–1977)

Sallie ranks among the earliest appointed missionaries of the United Pentecostal Church. She began her missionary work in Colombia just a few months after her appointment, according to the June 1948 *Pentecostal Herald*. She was appointed at the 1948 UPCI General Conference and arrived on Colombian soil in December 1948.[7] Sallie was best known as a soulwinner. She felt passionate about door-to-door evangelism, street meetings, and any other activities for reaching the lost. Her appointment to Colombia extended into 1956.

After eight years as a missionary in Colombia, a remarkable event changed her name and location; she married Missionary Lewis Morley, who was serving in Venezuela. Sallie had first met Lewis after he moved to Canada from England in 1930, but they had gone their separate ways.[8] Sallie labored in Colombia, and Lewis in Venezuela.

Daniel Scott wrote this description of Sallie and Lewis: “They say that opposites attract, and this was certainly the case when Lewis Morley, a witty Englishman, met Sallie Lemons, a very quiet, serious-minded American.

Obviously, the will of God brought them together."[9] They married in the late summer of 1956 at Pentecostal Tabernacle in Kingston, Jamaica, with plans to locate in Venezuela. Missionary Janet Varnado (Trout), a missionary in Jamaica with her parents, described their wedding:

> Two of our very fine missionaries, Sallie Lemons and Lewis Morley, were united in marriage on Thanksgiving Day at the Pentecostal Tabernacle in Kingston, Jamaica, by Brother A. D. Varnado, Missionary [to] Jamaica, and pastor of the church there. Brother V. A. Guidroz, Superintendent of the Texas District, visiting in Jamaica at the time, gave the bride away. Sister Janet Varnado served Sister Lemons as her maid of honor. Brother Edgar Eason, the first [believer] Brother Varnado baptized after arriving in Jamaica last year, was the best man. The church was decorated very simply with palms and roses. The bride carried a bouquet of white roses, which she made up herself. As the couple knelt at the altar at the end of the ceremony, Sister Janet Varnado sang "The Lord's Prayer."
>
> The presence of God was very real during the entire wedding. After the wedding, the happy couple spent a brief honeymoon about fifty miles from Kingston. One week and a day after their wedding, they boarded a plane back to their field of labor. They went first to Barranquilla, Colombia, and spent the weekend there with Brother and Sister [Verner] Larsen. They then went on to Valera, Venezuela, their present field of labor together.

As a single woman missionary and as a wife, Sallie lived frugally to devote everything possible to the work of soulwinning. They had no washing machine, fan, automobile, sewing machine, or refrigerator. The Morleys saved a thousand dollars from offerings received toward a new church building.[10] After working in Venezuela for two years after their marriage, the Morleys moved to Colombia to oversee the work established by Bill Drost. From 1958 to 1977, the work expanded to become one of the most productive works in UPCI history during those years.[11]

The Morleys retired from missions in 1977 but not from ministry. They worked with C. L. Dees in Houston, Texas, to minister among Latin American people.[12] In 1985, Sallie flew back to Colombia to participate in the ribbon-cutting and dedication ceremonies for the training facilities developed by Sidney Perdue, The Center for Pentecostal Bible Instruction in Cali. In 1988, they moved to Miami, Florida, to help establish three Spanish works among the many Colombians living there. Lewis passed away on March 28, 1997, at age eighty-two.[13]

Single again after the death of Lewis, Sallie returned to Colombia with her adopted Colombian son, Arley, who had promised Lewis he would take care of his mother, whose Alzheimer's disease was preventing her from living independently. However, her physical limitations did not rob her of her love for soulwinning. Arley took his mother to a Colombian park or neighborhood every day to pass out tracts and invite people to church. Though other mental tasks faded, Sallie's evangelism desires remained strong.

Ann Suarez, who ministered in the Latin world with her husband, Rito, who later opened a Spanish church in Chicago, wrote about Sallie's influential ministry:

In Sallie Morley's presence, I was convicted of the need to influence others for the kingdom of God. If I cowered in Sallie Morley's presence, how much more would I tremble when I stood before God? I knew then that I could not meet Him empty handed. Hispanic women need to be part of the "Women of the Word" army of soulwinners! The Bible studies [studies Sallie wrote during her missionary years] are a tool that will help get the job done.[14]

PART V
Europe / Middle East

17

Portugal, France, Morocco, Algeria, Tunisia

Elizabeth Andrade, Trecina Anderson, Kathy Miller

Portugal

Elizabeth Andrade (1976 self-supporting; appointed 1982–1989)

"What would you do if you were a widowed senior citizen who recognized a need in the land of her forefathers? If you were Elizabeth Andrade, you would pack your bags and move to Portugal." This is exactly what Elizabeth Andrade did in 1976, as stated in the *1984 Foreign Missions Story*. Born on June 17, 1915, Elizabeth was sixty-one when she began missionary work in Portugal. In the absence of a resident missionary, she labored faithfully and looked after the church in Lisbon. In 1982, she was officially appointed to Portugal as an assistant missionary.

Though twenty-first-century Apostolics may not have heard about Elizabeth, they may know about her daughter and grandson. Her daughter, Rachel Hattabaugh, once served as a missionary in Argentina, South America, with her husband, John. Her grandson, Mark Hattabaugh, who pastors in Cooper City, Florida, is well known in the UPCI fellowship as a member of the Global Missions Board, and for his ministry to Missionary Kids and Compassion Services International.

Rachel shared the following details about her remarkable mother:

> At the age of thirteen, Elizabeth lost her mother, and about two years later, she lost her father. Left without her parents, she married at a young age. Tragically, she was widowed at age twenty-seven with three children, ages five, four, and two. Along with caring for her young children, she dedicated her life to winning souls to the Lord. Her only desire was to be used by God wherever God would lead her.
>
> The Lord laid it on her heart to open a storefront church in New Bedford, Massachusetts, an hour's drive from her home in Providence, Rhode Island. Of Portuguese descent, she felt led to reach out to the Portuguese people in New Bedford. Her children helped her with painting and getting the building ready for services.
>
> One night she felt a strong burden to reach out to someone and did not get any release. She began driving, not knowing where she was going but seeking the Lord's guidance. When she ended up in New Bedford, she spotted a gentleman walking down a lonely street and felt impressed to talk to him. She rolled down her window and spoke to him, explaining that she didn't know him, but the Lord had sent her to tell him about His love. She said, "No matter what you are going through right now, God wants to help you. Can I pray for you?" He was indeed desperate, sharing that he had lost his job, and his wife wanted out of their marriage. He admitted he had nothing to live for and had been contemplating

suicide as he walked. After praying, Elizabeth gave him the storefront address where she held services. He came to the services and gave his heart to the Lord. God restored his marriage and blessed him with a better job. Instead of losing his life to suicide, he lived to see his whole family get saved.

After living and ministering in Massachusetts, Elizabeth moved to California to be near her brother. She hailed a taxi on a Sunday morning and told the driver she did not have an address but was looking for a Pentecostal church. He had not previously had such a request, but she was determined to find a Pentecostal church. As he drove up and down the streets of Los Angeles, she shared the gospel with him and prayed they would find a church. She didn't mind that the meter continued ticking because she enjoyed talking about the Lord to a hungry soul. At last they found a UPCI church! The pastor was John Flowers. The driver noted the address and told Elizabeth he would love to visit the church with his family. Never before had he heard of the loving God about whom she talked.

As it turned out, the taxi driver did attend the church with his family. They loved the worship and friendliness of the people. God touched their hungry hearts, and they became Pentecostals. Rachel added this note: "To this day, he [the taxi driver] pastors a United Pentecostal Church. Hallelujah!"

While living in California, Elizabeth got a job working for a wealthy family. She lived frugally and saved her earnings because she felt a calling to the country of Portugal. Though she did not receive an appointment through UPCI Foreign Missions, she felt strongly she had to go. She finalized plans to go to Portugal using funds from her meager Social Security check and the money saved from her California job. She arrived in Portugal just as Missionary Domingues was preparing to return to the States. To save money and brush up on speaking Portuguese, she lived with a family, serving as their maid. She cleaned the house, washed clothes by hand, and never complained, feeling that her work was all part of saying yes to the Lord's calling.

After four years in Portugal, Elizabeth returned to the States and met the Foreign Missions Board. In October 1982, she received her appointment. How happy she was! She served a total of thirteen years in Portugal.

After living back in the States, Elizabeth felt a calling to the Cape Verde Islands, the original home of her ancestors. These islands had no Apostolic church. As she made plans to go there to share the gospel, she contacted her grandson, Mark Hattabaugh. Mark had worked in Portugal with his grandmother before the AIM program had been developed. While working under his grandmother's supervision, he had learned Portuguese. Mark was delighted to accompany his grandmother to Cape Verde. The trip to Cape Verde for Mark was both exciting and disappointing.

Mark and his grandmother flew to Portugal. When the time came for them to travel by boat to Cape Verde, they made their way to the dock with boxes of tracts and their suitcases. Their fellow travelers included drunken passengers and smelly animals. They went to the capital city on one of the islands, and from there caught a cargo boat to the island where Elizabeth felt God had called her. This boat was also filled with animals and drunken passengers, and booze had been packed in every possible space. Since the boat had no designated seating, Elizabeth found a spot on a narrow bench. She felt very uncomfortable when a drunk seated himself next to her. Mark found a place to lie down on a net covering the cargo.

While on the boat, Mark inquired about a return boat trip to Portugal to catch his flight back to the States. He learned that the next boat back would not be until a week later. If he wanted to be on the return flight, he had no other choice but to stay on the boat and leave his grandmother alone on the dock with her tracts and suitcase. That was a sad day for Mark.

Elizabeth found a hotel, but it was infested with flies and ants. She got rid of the ants, but the flies remained. At the restaurant, she had to clean the leftover food residue off her plate before she could eat. She stayed on the island for six months, sharing the good news of the gospel with everyone she met. Her ministry introduced the Apostolic message to Cape Verde Island. Due to sickness, she had to return to the States. Today, the island has a strong work pastored by missionaries from Brazil.

Elizabeth Andrade spent her last days in Arvin, California. Her daughter Rachel, who was living in San Diego at the time, was planning to attend a wedding near her mother's home. She mentioned the wedding to her mother and asked if she wanted to attend as well. Excited about seeing her daughter,

> Elizabeth agreed to attend the wedding. Elizabeth, who lived four hours from her family, had rejected the idea of moving closer to them, expressing that they probably would be moving again.

The conclusion of Elizabeth's story speaks volumes about her relationship with the Lord. She had always observed a 5:00 AM prayer time every morning. In her morning prayer before attending the wedding, she asked the Lord to take her "home" while Rachel was there. After the wedding, they changed clothes and decided to go out for a Mexican dinner. As Rachel was backing the car out, her mother said, "Wait, let me leave my purse in the house; I won't need it where I am going." At the restaurant Elizabeth put hot sauce on enchiladas and asked Rachel if she wanted some. They prayed over their food. Then the unexpected happened; Elizabeth suffered a fatal heart attack. She went to her heavenly home, leaving her purse behind. Rachel shared these words about her mother's sudden passing.

> She had her early morning talk with her Lord and asked Him to take her while her daughter was there. Her faithful Lord answered her last prayer. Mom always said, "God is faithful," and He was till the very end. What a dedication, love, and devotion to the Lord, whom she served and loved! God called, and she answered His call. She called Him to take her home, and our faithful God answered.

Elizabeth passed away on July 20, 1996, the month before her eighty-first birthday.[1]

Spain and Portugal

Trecina Anderson (2011 to Spain; 2015–2023 to Portugal)

What should one think if she were seeking direction from the Lord about her ministry calling, and the Lord's repeated answer was the word for *trees* in Spanish? Trecina Anderson, a Jamaican who had emigrated to the United States, did not know what to think of the Lord's answer. She was having a vision at the altar and heard herself say the Spanish word for "trees." At that time, Trecina did not know how to speak Spanish.

Trecina had been in the church for several years and had fully committed her life to the Lord by the age of eighteen. She was attending Florida Atlantic University, pursuing her childhood dream of becoming a journalist, when she felt her call to the ministry. She had returned to Jamaica for a convention, and at the altar the Lord had transformed her desires into His desires. While praying in tongues, she said in her spirit, "I will not work for men, but I will work for God."[2]

When she returned to her church in West Palm Beach, Florida, her pastor, Daniel R. Kyle, advised her not to quit college but to seek God to know His specific calling. She started a campus ministry at her university and saw a great revival there. That was the beginning of Trecina's ministry.

As Trecina continued to seek direction from the Lord, she attended a youth event in Gainesville, Florida, and saw a vision of a landscape opening before her, followed by the aforementioned repetition of the Spanish word for *trees*. She did not understand the vision, but the Lord moved on the preacher Jason Sciscoe to return to the microphone and proclaim that the Lord had revealed a part of someone's vision to him. He said a person in the auditorium had a vision of a landscape, and the Lord wanted the person to know He was calling that person not just to visit the mission field, but to be a missionary. This message was important, because Trecina was planning to go on a Youth on Missions (YOM) trip to Spain and Portugal in just five months. The message also made clear what her calling to the ministry was, but the significance of the word *trees* had not yet been revealed.

Two months before her YOM trip, Trecina attended a Ladies Retreat in Ocala, Florida, where she began speaking in tongues in fluent Spanish. She recalled that special time: "The day I spoke in tongues during the prayer meeting, I was simply glorifying the Lord in Spanish. I don't remember what the words were, because at that time I didn't understand Spanish, but I knew I was blessing the Lord."[3] From this, she inferred that her future field of labor might be in a Spanish-speaking country.

Trecina had yet to learn there were many Spanish-speaking countries. She had heard of missionaries who started in one country and ended up in another, so she asked the Lord to let her know where to begin. During prayer at age twenty-one, after her first overseas trip, the Lord again gave her direction through a Spanish word. This time it was the Spanish word for Spain: *España*.

To learn Spanish, Trecina spent her last semester in college doing a study-abroad program at the University of Salamanca in Salamanca, Spain. With the Lord's help, she was speaking Spanish within three months. During her time in Salamanca, she connected with a UPCI family from Madrid, the Ignacio Cortez family, who were trying to start a church in Salamanca. The first Bible studies in Spanish that Trecina taught were there in Salamanca.

After graduating from college, Trecina applied for the Associate in Missions program in Spain. Following a year of fundraising, she began her missionary career under the supervision of Missionary Gary D. Sones in Madrid in 2004, where she also attended the Bible college. After helping in the work in Spain for several terms as an AIMer, Trecina was granted her missionary appointment to the country of Spain at the 2011 UPCI General Conference. After one full term as an appointed missionary, she received a call in 2015 from Missionary William Markham, who had been in Portugal for twenty-five years. He told Trecina they needed her to come to Portugal.

She transferred to Portimão, Portugal, in the southern part of the country. A short time later, on a car ride up to Lisbon to preach in William Markham's church, she finally understood the significance of the Spanish word for *trees* that the Lord had given her years before at the altar in Gainesville, Florida. Everywhere Trecina looked there were fields and fields of trees. She learned that Portugal is one of only three countries where cork oak trees grow and that Portugal is the world's leading cork producer. This confirmed the part of the vision that she had not understood all those years ago. Her time in Spain had been a time of preparation for her labor in Portugal, the country of the trees.

Within one year of Trecina's transfer from Spain to the work in Portugal, William Markham died, but the Lord had already put into place one of the people who would carry on the work. Trecina was there mastering a new language—Portuguese.

Trecina offers some insightful advice. "If you feel a call to do something for God, don't feel afraid, or that you are not prepared or not good enough, or that you are unable to do it. Just do it! God is faithful. He will help you and will open doors for you and take care of you."[4]

Trecina's other bit of advice for anyone determined to work for the Lord was birthed from a message she heard the late Eli Hernandez preach just before she left for Portugal. She urges, "As when Nehemiah was rebuilding the wall and the enemy was trying to hinder the work, when your enemy tries to work against what you are trying to do for the Lord, it is just a distraction to prevent you from seeing the victory the Lord is already bringing. Go to the Lord and ask Him to strengthen your hands (Nehemiah 6:9). Get on your knees and speak in tongues, for that is the Holy Ghost speaking through you!"[5]

France, Morocco, Algeria, and Tunisia

Kathy Miller (1982–2003)

Kathy Miller studied nursing at the University of Washington and then worked at the Seattle Children's Hospital before she began two decades of missionary life. Kathy moved from Washington State to France in 1982 to assist the Nowackis (UPCI missionaries) with their children's education. While serving on this AIM assignment, Kathy earned two master's degrees from the University of Paris. Almost twelve years later, in September 1994, she was appointed as a UPCI missionary to France. Her call to France dates back to 1981, when she felt the Lord telling her to give her life for His service in France. In early 1997, she completed her deputation and returned to France.[6]

While teaching the Nowacki children during her AIM years, she developed an evangelistic ministry through home Bible studies and home visits. Returning to France, she opened the first United Pentecostal Church in Southeast France in Toulon and established preaching points in Grenoble in the French Alps and Aix-en-Provence. In addition to her pastoral ministry, she taught full-time in the French Bible school.[7]

In January 1999, she was diagnosed with emphysema and advised to relocate to a more suitable climate. In considering her health issues and a burden for Muslims, she requested a move to North Africa. Thus, in April 1999, the Foreign Missions Board approved her field change to Morocco, Algeria, and Tunisia.[8] Kathy served in Morocco, Algeria, and Tunisia from October 1999 to May 2003. She resigned due to health issues.

Back in the US, she worked with the North Cities United Pentecostal Church in Garland, Texas, as a minister and school principal from August 2003 to May 2009. Since 2009, she has taught French in three different Texas high schools.

18

Switzerland and Russia

Amber Hackenbruch, Janice Hersey

Switzerland

Amber Hackenbruch (2009–Active)

Amber Hackenbruch penned her story about how God had directed her into missionary work before she reached her teen years. Here is Amber's story with minor editorial adaptations.

When I was twelve, God dropped the idea of missions into my heart and mind. It was New Year's Eve 2001 at Life Church in Anchorage, Alaska. I remember so clearly because of the banners I can still see on the wall in my mind's eye. The banner on the left wall of the sanctuary said, "Breakthrough 2002." More important, though, the banner hanging from the ceiling read, "What would you attempt for God if you knew you couldn't fail?"

That was the message my pastor asked us to consider as he preached that night. Toward the end of the service, he passed out little blank slips of paper and instructed us to take a few moments in prayer to ask the Lord to put a bigger dream in us than we could accomplish on our own. We weren't supposed to analyze our response or try to find all the answers; our only responsibility was to listen and then write down what the Lord said. The rest was up to God.

That service took place over twenty years ago. Since then, the Lord has opened ministry doors in Austria, Switzerland, and Germany. Since 2009, God has allowed me to serve His kingdom in established churches, in new church plants in cities without an Apostolic preacher, in Bible schools, home Bible studies, evangelism, and so much more. God has allowed me to see miracles of healing, divine protection, great outpourings of His Spirit, and the revelation of the mighty God in Christ in countless locations.

Specifically, I'll never forget the wave of the revelation of truth that our missionary and national team witnessed in the German-speaking nations. Until 2015, our primary focus was building leaders locally and nationally through our Bible school programs, the Apostolic Ministry Training Center (AMTC) and Purpose Institute (PI).

Everything changed, and Kingdom work went into overdrive when God divinely connected us with an unaffiliated, charismatic minister named David Gaziala. While David was living in Israel, God had connected him with UPCI Missionary Robert McFarland. David Gaziala moved to Germany in 2015. Shortly after that, he contacted Missionary Charles Robinette in Vienna, Austria, who was serving as the general superintendent of the German-Speaking Nations (GSN). Through this connection, David Gaziala received the revelation of Apostolic truth, and he immediately began building bridges to other unaffiliated ministers across the GSN to facilitate the revelation of truth for them as well.

By the end of 2020, AMTC campuses were operating in over thirty unaffiliated churches throughout Austria, Switzerland, and Germany. UPCI missionaries were rebaptizing large numbers of saints, ministers, and pastors in the mighty name of Jesus! Hundreds were being filled with the Holy Ghost in churches that UPCI ministers never planted. The ripples of this wave of revelation continue to this day. Many of these unaffiliated ministers have continued to preach this Apostolic message from their pulpits, and some have even become licensed ministers in the UPC GSN.

This unprecedented harvest in the GSN was not what I pictured as a girl in Anchorage, Alaska. It would not have included living on foreign soil if I had planned my life. I certainly wouldn't have imagined that God would have me preaching in pulpits. It would have been so easy to remain inside the lines of a life I could imagine. If you would have asked me if I wanted to be a single missionary, I couldn't have fathomed that reality. The idea of the isolation and challenge such a calling brings would have been enough to keep me safe at home.

Thank God He didn't let me in on the whole plan. He still doesn't. Instead, He leads me from my comfort zone one little step at a time. At a young age, He put a dream in my heart that stabilized me and caused me to thrive in His kingdom through all the challenges I encountered along this journey. I have learned that you can accomplish anything in the kingdom of God when you know that the dream wasn't originally your idea. By holding on to the promises of God, we become His hands by which He will reap His end-time harvest. There is no place I would rather be than in His field, which is currently Switzerland.[1]

Russia

Janice Hersey (2002–2006)

Janice Hersey was among the twenty newly appointed missionaries introduced at the 2002 UPCI General Conference. She received her full appointment at age twenty-three, becoming one of the youngest women appointed by the UPCI. William Turner, a veteran missionary to

Russia, told her story in his book, *The Church on Godless Lane: Missionary Stories from Russia and the Former Soviet Union.* Janice resigned from her appointment in August 2011 due to health reasons.

With William Turner's permission, details and quotes from his book tell Janice's story as a missionary.

> Janice came by her zeal for ministry and her burden for foreign missions at an early age. Her father, David Hersey, was for many years a pastor and the Foreign Missions director in the Maine District. . . . Janice began studying the Russian language at age fifteen and later graduated from Gateway College in Florissant, Missouri. Soon afterward, she volunteered for the Associates in Missions program in St. Petersburg, Russia, under the missionary oversight of Tim and Jane Olson. Early on, she roomed with two Russian young ladies from the St. Petersburg church, generally speaking only Russian in their apartment. Within a year or two, her basic Russian skills developed into true fluency. With the eagerness of a sharp intelligence and a passion to reach the Russian people, she became the most proficient linguist among the missionaries in the former Soviet Union.[2]
>
> Following her appointment in 2002, Janice continued working another year in the church in St. Petersburg while awaiting a deputation schedule in North America. During her deputation, Missionary Turner discussed options for her ministry in Russia. One extremely challenging option was opening a new work in Kazan, located about five hundred miles east of Moscow. Kazan is the capital of

Tatarstan, a semi-autonomous republic within the Russian Federation. Muslims and ethnic Tatars (an ethnic group related to the Mongols who conquered Russia in the thirteenth century) comprise over 50 percent of the population. Knowing the possible difficulties, Janice chose the option of Kazan, ready to make a long-term commitment to the area. Then unexpected health issues restricted Janice's time in Kazan to just over one year. Perhaps her season there was for the eternal benefit of just one soul.[3]

Two years before the arrival of Janice Hersey in Kazan, a young Russian woman born in that city applied for an opening posted at her local university, a summer job at a Jewish community center in Wisconsin. She was accepted and found herself working with American volunteers in the city of Wisconsin Dells. Her name was Elena Shanskaya. She soon struck up a friendship with a local Pentecostal, Marybeth Neinast. Elena became a frequent visitor in the Neinast home. That friendship with Marybeth and Dale Neinast opened a door of biblical revelation and spiritual discovery for her that Elena had never known existed. This was completely amazing and totally life-changing for that young Russian university student.

Out of deference to her friends, Elena began attending services at Turnpoint Pentecostal Church in Wisconsin Dells, and, for the first time in her life, heard a message of salvation she had not known was in the Bible. . . . In America, she heard about and read the Book of Acts for the first time. When Elena returned to the US the following summer, her own personal prayer and Bible study made her increasingly receptive to what Marybeth had shared the previous year. During her second summer in America, she accepted the Neinasts' invitation to live in their home. They had become her American "mom and dad."[4]

Elena's continued attendance at Turnpoint Church ultimately reached her heart. She found herself longing to experience God's touch. At the end of a service, she joined others at the altar and decided to be baptized in the name of Jesus Christ. With Marybeth's encouragement and instruction, she prayed to be filled with the Spirit. God answered Elena's prayer just a few weeks before her return to Russia. While living in the Neinasts' home, Elena learned by example the importance of reading God's Word and praying. One day when Marybeth entered the house, she heard the sounds of travailing prayer. Elena's voice wafted up from the lower level as she prayed in Russian and in tongues. Marybeth stopped in the kitchen, feeling the urge to lie on the floor to join Elena in prayer. When Elena's voice grew quiet, Marybeth went down the stairs. They embraced, and Elena announced, "Mom, I must go back to Russia and tell the people there about what God has revealed to me."[5]

A few months after Elena's return to Kazan to continue her university studies, the Turners visited the Wisconsin Dells church on their deputation and heard Elena's story. Soon after, William emailed Elena, knowing she had no Apostolic church to attend. (She was attending a Baptist church for Christian fellowship.) She completed her studies and began management training in a European home furnishings store. A year went by without Elena having any Apostolic fellowship.

Janice Hersey was back in St. Petersburg as an appointed missionary by this time. However, she was still deciding where she could be the most effective in ministry. Missionary Turner mentioned Kazan again as a possible place for opening a new work, knowing that Elena would be a willing helper. After prayer and consultation with Regional Director Robert Rodenbush, Janice committed to opening a work in Kazan. When Janice moved to Kazan, she shared an apartment with Elena, and together they held Bible studies in their apartment.

Just as Janice and Elena seemed close to reaping a harvest from their Bible teaching, Janice began to develop health problems: migraines and then progressive dizziness and disorientation. As her condition worsened, she found it necessary to return to the States for a detailed physical examination. On the way back to the US, she stopped off in Holland for the European Conference, where she did an outstanding job interpreting for the speaker. Her excellent command of Russian was an instrument in blessing the fellowship of the EME [Europe/Middle East] Region.

The results of Janice's physical examination came as shocking news. The tests revealed a benign tumor at the base of the brain, which could continue to grow and intensify her problems. Surgery was not a simple option because chances were great for damage from any surgery, including loss of hearing, vision, and even mobility. Janice made only one return visit to Kazan, with the help of her brother, to settle her affairs and pack her belongings for shipment back home. Back in the States, she found it necessary to apply for permanent disability.

Janice spent only one year in Kazan. William Turner expressed that God's ways are above man's ways. Perhaps Janice's one year in Kazan provided a crucial stabilizing factor in the life of a committed Russian Apostolic. Soon after Janice left Kazan, Elena's employer transferred her to Moscow and St. Petersburg. In these cities, she continued her spiritual growth as a member of Apostolic churches. During that time, Elena renewed her friendship with a young man, Ramon, whom she had known while attending the university. She invited him to church, and in time, he was baptized and filled with the Holy Ghost. At the time of [William's] writing, Ramon and Elena were employed in Moscow and [were attending] the UPC church. They married in 2009 and have remained active in the Moscow church.[6]

19

Jordan and an Access-Challenged Nation

Cynthia White, Nancy Mansfield, Bonnie L.

Jordan

Cynthia White (February 2010-May 2014)

When Cynthia White was born on December 9, 1973, in Glasgow, Kentucky, to Joe and Sharon White, her parents could not have known she would become a missionary. In her childhood, Cyndy moved to Taylorville, Illinois, where she graduated from high school in 1991. She then attended Indiana Bible College (IBC) and Missouri Baptist University, earning degrees in education and theology.

With a heart for missions, Cyndy spent two weeks in Malawi, Africa, in the mid-1990s at the invitation of a fellow IBC student, Jason Crumpacker, who had grown up in Africa as a missionary kid. Jason's memories of Cyndy include her excellent musical talent, outgoing, friendly personality, and contagious laughter.[1]

After her trip to Africa, Cyndy began making missions trips as an associate in missions to Jordan, where Gary and Linda Reed (her aunt and uncle) served as missionaries. She would stay in Jordan for around nine months and then return to the States to raise funds. In Jordan, she assisted Linda Reed and distributed clothing and food to the needy through the church. She also taught English as a second language.

After serving intermittently as an AIMer for over ten years, Cyndy received her missionary appointment to

Jordan in February 2010. During her deputation, Cyndy saved portions of her offerings as part of her budget, thus shortening her deputation time. This concept influenced the creation of "I Am Global" offerings at the UPCI General Conferences. In assisting the Reeds, she helped start several churches and then became the pastor of the Filipino church.[2]

Cyndy's sister, Michelle Hancock, shared some insights about Cyndy from people in Jordan who were touched by her life and ministry. One individual wrote that "she loved people easy" and had a big compassion for Filipinos and Sri Lankans. Another person said she always helped and loved all kinds of people—young, old, and babies. She was always happily ready to serve the Lord while encouraging and supporting others. She loved the Arab people. In relating to different cultures, she would try any food, commenting that if others could eat it, she could too.[3]

During her years in missionary work, Cyndy coped courageously with severe diabetes and still forged ahead to fulfill her dream of being a missionary. She passed away unexpectedly on May 16, 2014, at the age of forty in Amman, Jordan, due to health issues. Her obituary states that she was an avid sesquipedalian (a person who uses big words). Cyndy knew how to use big words and do big things for the kingdom of God.

Nancy Mansfield (AIM 2011 / Appointment 2016–Active)

Nancy Mansfield, a missionary appointed to the Hashemite Kingdom of Jordan, was born in Texas in June 1990. Her parents raised her in the house of God, where she received the Holy Spirit and was baptized at the age of six. Nancy likes to say that she received her calling to ministry from her mother. Anytime the church doors were open, her family was there to do whatever needed doing. "You never say no if you are asked to do something for the church" was a well-known commandment in her home. However, as is often the case, being present in the church building did not always equate with being genuinely connected with God.

Nancy describes the years of her youth as a decade where her only times of sincere prayer and consecration were at the altar during church services or prayer meetings. She describes herself as becoming an attitude-prone, hard-hearted young lady who found herself straying farther away from God. It was in this state that Nancy received her call to missions. This is the account of that event in her own words:

> When I was seventeen, a friend talked me into going to a senior youth camp, quite against my will. I watched that same friend lying prostrate at the altar after service, with tears rolling down her cheeks. My heart seemed as hard as a callus; I just sat on the pew watching her. Her tears must have softened my heart a little because I eventually surrendered to prayer. I knew I could not lie on the floor and weep as she did. I didn't have it in me to give that to God yet. So I just put my head in my hands and said, "God, whatever You want me to do, I'll do it." God promptly spoke into my spirit, "Foreign Missions" (now called Global Missions). I had never thought of doing missionary work. I had seen missionaries come and go. I had even been overseas, but missionary work had never been on

my radar. From that moment, however, I knew I would be a missionary.

Knowing she would need training in the basics of Scripture and missions work, Nancy attended Bible college in Texas, where she majored in missions. She went on a two-month Next Steps trip to the Dominican Republic during summer break and a three-week trip to Trinidad to teach vacation Bible school. Knowing that God had called her to be a missionary, she knew that after Bible college she should apply to the AIM program for a longer trip. She decided to go to Scotland in 2011 for her first AIM term, where she received much-needed training in the administration of the Bible school. During her time in Scotland, Nancy visited a Muslim nation for the first time. At the insistence of Missionary Jerolyn Kelley, Nancy went on a prayer trip to Turkey. She shares key memories from that trip:

> We flew into Istanbul during the darkest part of the night. However, as I gazed out the plane window, it looked like every light in the city was on. I remember thinking, *They are trying so hard to push back the darkness*. During this trip was the first time I saw hundreds of Muslims kneeling to pray in the street. The sight brought me to tears and still does. Our little group brought the presence of God into those streets as we walked, sang, and prayed through the city. Little did I know that this short prayer trip would be a small glimpse into the future of my ministry in missions.

At the end of Nancy's term in Scotland, the EME regional director asked if she would be willing to go to Jordan for four months. Nancy recalls that she didn't even know the location of Jordan. A month later—after prayer and a few letters sent back to the States for financing—Nancy found herself leaving rainy Scotland for the deserts of Jordan. Jordan offered a different kind of training for Nancy as she became the personal assistant of veteran missionary Linda Reed. During her initial four-month trip to Jordan in the summer of 2012, Nancy helped to start the work in Zarqa, Jordan (which would eventually become where she lived and pastored).

She left Jordan at the end of four months with an open invitation to return to continue helping Missionary Reed. In Nancy's mind, however, she was waiting for her "Macedonian call." Nancy had heard of missionaries having dreams or visions of where God wanted them to go, and she wanted her own vision. So after she returned to the States, she was determined not to go on any more missions trips until God revealed to her the nation of her calling. In her words, it was "a miserable three months."

Finally, when the misery reached its height, her pastor preached, "When you don't know what to do, do what you know to do." She didn't know where she was called but knew she was called to missions. She determined then to go wherever she was needed until God told her otherwise. Nancy returned to Jordan in 2013 and continued to serve there until the regional director suggested she apply for intermediate missionary status in 2016. She was fully appointed at the General Conference that year and has continued to serve in Jordan until the present time. Even though Nancy's calling to missions was clear, God chose to direct her to her country of calling through the guidance of church-appointed leaders. Nancy feels secure in her calling to Jordan, as expressed in her own words:

> I wished God would have spelled out where He desired me to be. That would have been a lot easier for me. I simply went where I was asked to go by my leadership. Then somewhere along the way I realized I hoped they would never ask me to go anywhere else. I remember thinking, "If they ask me to leave Jordan, I will be devastated." That's when I knew God had indeed called and sent me to Jordan. He had given me a love for this nation and these people, and there was no other place on earth that I would rather serve."

Access Challenged Nation (ACN)

Bonnie L. (AIM 2008 / Appointment May 2023–Active)

Bonnie grew up in Texas (Houston and Austin) in Apostolic churches. Her mother was a third-generation Apostolic, and her father became a first-generation Apostolic. She had known from her childhood that she would be a missionary. Her family recalls incidents of her weeping at the altar and telling them, "When I grow up, I'm going to be a missionary to Africa." She attended an Accelerated Christian Education (ACE) church school. After the family moved to Austin in her teen years, tragedy struck the core of her family. In this season of distress, Bonnie decided to live for God regardless of the family circumstances. She stood with truth and holiness and pursued God's call on her life, which led to her involvement in AIM trips and getting licensed with the UPCI.

At age eighteen, Bonnie began her missionary journey in 2008 as an associate in missions. She served twice in Vanuatu and once in Botswana. In 2011, Bonnie served as a furlough replacement on the island of Espiritu Santo, Vanuatu, where she ran the literacy school. During this time of short-term missions, she felt lacking in many areas—"spiritual disciplines, motivation, a good theology core of knowledge, a hard work ethic, and knowing how to serve others as Christ would."[4] Recognizing her limitations, Bonnie returned to the States and attended Urshan College in Missouri.

In 2019, Bonnie committed to serving full-time in Global Missions as an AIMer. She had been serving in Jordan for about ten months when COVID hit and necessitated her return to the States. When the pandemic began to subside in the second half of 2020, Bonnie went to Europe to serve in Latvia and worked there until March 2022. She then moved back to the Middle East. After working in Oman, Jordan, for about four months, she was diagnosed with ovarian cancer. Miraculously, after surgery and a biopsy that indicated there were no further areas of concern, she was cleared to go back to her normal life.

During the waiting time, Bonnie applied for an upgrade from the Associated Minister Program in Oman, Jordan, to appointment as an intermediate missionary to two access-challenged nations. She envisions working with the Kurdish people and other unreached groups in these areas. To Bonnie's delight, she was approved for appointment in May 2023. During the 2023 summer months, she worked in Oman with the Apostello group and representatives on the ground. At the time of this writing, she awaits the beginning of her deputation in January 2024.[5]

20

An Unfinished Story

The previous chapters provide glimpses into the lives of more than fifty single women who have served as appointed missionaries of the United Pentecostal Church International. The ministries of these single Apostolic women have touched every corner of the world. In compiling this history, we acknowledge that some missionaries may have been overlooked due to insufficient information. We sincerely thank Janice Leaman, who has repeatedly searched the records to help locate and clarify information about single lady missionaries of the UPCI. As this book demonstrates, single women have made vital contributions to the spread of the Apostolic message worldwide.

Single Women in Short-term Missions in 2023

Single women missionary stories will continue, for many of these stories are unfinished. Ten women whose stories are in this book currently serve as appointed missionaries. The current team of single missionaries is significantly enlarged by the many single women who serve worldwide in Short-Term Missions, including AIM (Associates in Missions), AMP (Associated Minister Program), Next Steps (a two-month program), and Apostello attendees. (See the afterword for a detailed description of Global Missions' short-term mission programs.) In August 2023, single women in short-term missions numbered 174 out of 347, or 50 percent of the short-term missionaries. This number includes anyone who serves in missions for two-plus months and whose time on the field counts toward applying for higher levels of missions.

As a fitting conclusion to this history of single women missionaries, we share the story of a widowed missionary—now a single AIMer—who has never quit.

Sharon Ikerd (AIM in Africa, 2011–Active)

Those who have followed Global Missions reports through the years will recognize the names of veteran missionaries Donald and Sharon Ikerd, who served as missionaries in Kenya, Zambia, and South Africa (1973–2002). Their story is told in *SENT! Volume 3, A History of UPCI Global Missions, Africa.* On their return to the States, the Ikerds pastored in Arizona. After pastoral ministry and a season of health issues, Donald passed away on January 25, 2008.

About three years after Don's passing, Sharon rejoined Global Missions (2011) as an AIMer to Africa. She first taught on the island of Mauritius for six months and then on the island of Rodrigues for three months. She then moved to Seychelles, where she taught in the Bible school for over two years and worked with the ladies to encourage church growth.

Sharon faced some health issues as she pursued her AIM assignments and had to spend time in the US for treatment and recovery; however, when she regained her strength, she returned to Africa to continue her missionary ministry. In 2021, I received an email from Sharon with this update:

> This finds me in Namibia on AIM. I teach GATS Bible School for the first and second-year classes and have Sunday morning Bible studies at home.

> The Lord has blessed me, and I love what I am doing. The Covid lockdowns have been challenging this year, but we made it. Thank the Lord! My first-year students just finished and are ready to graduate. I stay busy, as I also send out daily Scripture quotations and words of encouragement to all my students and those to whom I give Bible studies.

At the time of this writing, Sharon has devoted twelve years to missionary work as a single lady. She is not finished yet! The loss of her husband did not diminish her burden and missionary calling in her senior years. Her unwavering faith and steadfast labors provide an inspiring example for younger people sensing God's call to global missions.

We conclude with this: We hope and pray that many more single women will heed God's call to global missions and continue the story.

Afterword

Short-Term Missions: A Pathway to the Global Harvest by James Poitras Director of Education/Short-Term Missions

Short-term missions has developed into a pathway experienced by thousands since its inception over forty years ago. As we continue enlarging the trail for future generations, we recognize a mounting need to accommodate a wider diversity of endeavors fueled by an evangelistic fervor of those answering the call. Annually, more than nine hundred individuals are involved in one of our programs. A small, but determinedly dedicated, short-term team at UPCI World Headquarters is led by the director of education/short-term missions. The team is committed to missions mobilization, missions mentoring, missions program engineering, and empowering others to serve in the global harvest. We continue to create a community of laborers while providing a pathway to the harvest. This is our story; a history that is still being written.

Occasionally, I am asked if short-term missions is the priority or trend of Global Missions. There are various possibilities that come with trends. One can go with a trend, kick against a trend, or plan one's own trend. The persistent mission of the UPCI and Global Missions is to take the whole gospel to the whole world by the whole church. Did you notice that last little component—"by the whole church"? Everyone can be (and should be) involved in fulfilling the Great Commission. We can each be a global Christian, or "goer." We accomplish this through praying, giving, and going (or any variation thereof). No one in the church is exempted, so it stands to reason that the short-term missions programs of the UPCI should grow exponentially. It is part of the Master's master plan.

As the director of Global Missions short-term missions programs, I envision, along with our general director, a thousand or more people mobilized for overseas involvement each year. We are planning and preparing for that. Our trend, therefore, is to get as many as possible involved in traversing a pathway to the harvest and reaching the world. Our mission is that every tribe and nation will know the name of Jesus. The banner of the UPCI flies in 240 nations and territories of our world. The sun never sets on the United Pentecostal Church International, yet, reaching the world is far from accomplished with over seven thousand unreached people groups. We train the messengers, send them with the message, and nurture the churches. That is our mission, vision, objective, and purpose. In an ever-changing world where little seems constant, that message and that mission never waiver. They never change. When God desires to send His message, He wraps it in a messenger, and sends the messenger.

I spent twenty-eight years on the mission field before coming to World Headquarters. Writing these words, with tears forming, makes me want to jump up from this desk, and rush back into the harvest. If I could relive my life, I would do missions work and more missions work all over again. That is not an opportunity, so I will spend the rest of my life mentoring short-term missionaries for the mission. It is one of the best jobs on the planet.

Here is the trend from my perspective: let us get as many people involved in the harvest as possible. It is not all about short-term missions. It is about missions. Look at the missionary map. Notice anything in particular? We have an aging missionary team. Short-term missions efforts provide potential candidates for long-term missions. That is a major goal. In closing, I will describe some of the short-term missions programs presently available.

Apostolic Youth Corps (AYC): apostolicyouthcorps.com

A starting place in short-term missions is the Apostolic Youth Corps with UPCI Youth Ministries. Hundreds of young people each year travel to global and North American locations to experience grassroots, hands-on missions and endeavor to be a blessing. Although not administrated by Global Missions, we work with AYC each year to facilitate the trips to global locations.

Global ConNEXTions: global connextions.org

Established in 2016, Global ConNEXTions Weekend is a biennial interactive event, conveying the sights, sounds, and smells of global missions right here at home. It is an experience that connects those who have a desire to do global missions work with others who are on the same path, building a community of global Christians. Those who have participated in Apostolic Youth Corps, Youth on Mission, Next Steps, and church missions trips find this experience to be very edifying. Pastors and church leaders who want to develop a greater missions emphasis in their local church will find this experience inspiring and informational.

GoNEXT Kids

To continue to sow good seed into good soil, Global Missions seeks to begin the process of including the alpha generation in its missions scope. The alpha generation refers to those born since 2010. We are intent on mobilizing as many people in this group as possible to be global Christians. Why? Because global Christians pray for the lost and give their time, talents, and resources to care for others. And some are invited by the Lord of the harvest to serve as NEXT GEN missionaries.

Did you know that many of our current missionaries and AIMers experienced their call to missions between grades three and eight? With this in mind, GoNEXT Kids was created as an interactive missions experience designed to connect kids with an interest in or a call to missions with those in Global Missions. Training with missions prayer tools, international worship songs, missions group games, and other resources are available at the event.

TEFL/TESOL Certification: aim2go.org/tesol

Teaching English is a great way to spread the gospel at home and abroad, opening doors to communities that are often closed to the gospel. Short-term missions hosts one certification program each summer, accommodating fifteen to eighteen participants. Certificates are issued by the Teach2Go Network, a growing network of Apostolic certified ESL trainers. Candidates can earn a sixty or a one-hundred-hour certificate. Many use their certificates to help run English programs in their local church or to obtain employment while AIMing in a nation.

Going and taking your work with you is not restricted to TESL. You could be the key to unlocking the door to a "closed" or "access-challenged" nation with the gospel. The global marketplace could be a seedbed for church growth. You can go into all the world and take your education and work expertise with you. Your educational experience, in God's will and timing, could be the catalyst launching you into a new angle on missions.

Associated Ministers: gmstm.net/am

Associated ministers are an integral part of the missions mobilization initiatives of the UPCI Global Missions short-term missions community. Any licensed minister in good standing with their district who can provide three positive references may apply. Approval gives the minister global missions status and serves as an outlet for reports as well as a connection point for short-term missions updates.

Advanced Global Educators: gmstm.net/get and gatsonline.org/get

The primary focus of the advanced global educators is to train the trainers. UPCI Global Missions has over 550 training centers outside of the United States and Canada. Many of these are part of our flagship theological education program, the Global Association of Theological Studies (GATS). The GATS program hosts dozens of two- to three-day faculty development programs around the globe, using their advanced global educators series. Such development programs require instructors who are academically qualified, doctrinally sound, culturally relevant, financially stable, and missionally driven. You may be a perfect fit for our team!

Advanced global educators facilitate these faculty education programs and can also be involved in short, intensified bachelor level courses offered through GATS and the Global University of Theological Studies. Some also help develop curriculum for overseas Bible schools and faculty education courses.

Next Steps Program: nextstepsprogram.net

The Next Steps Program, started in the early 2000s, continues to be a bridge between the AYC and AIM programs. Offering summer assignments lasting eight weeks, it is the perfect solution for hyphen-aged participants looking to spend more time on the field during school breaks. The program is divided into two segments: three weeks of training given by STM personnel and missionaries, and five weeks of apprenticing to be a missionary. We like to say it is three weeks of training for a lifetime of service. Each year a growing percentage of next steppers go on to be AIMers. We are now seeing many of those moving through our programs to become fully appointed missionaries. UPCI Youth Ministries through Sheaves for Christ allocates eight scholarships per year to qualifying youths who have been on AYC trips and are pursuing further missions participation. A similar program, Apostello, is offered each summer for those with experience on AIM, with a call and emphasis on reaching access-challenged nations.

Associates in Missions: aim2go.org

The Associates in Missions (AIM) program got its start in 1980 as a way to provide personnel to labor alongside missionaries and as a training ground for future missionaries. All around the world committed, missions-focused individuals are making a massive impact through involvement in part-time and full-time ministry. This includes working with churches, Bible schools, orphanages, and more.

Robert K. Rodenbush was appointed as the coordinator of Overseas Ministries in 1978 and launched the Associates in Missions (AIM program). Before the program was inaugurated in 1980, Global Missions did not have an established policy for short-term missions work. Prior to that time, there were efforts like assistant missionaries and a short-term Impact team that existed, but no formal policy had been created. Harry Scism tasked Brother Rodenbush with coming up with a short-term missions plan for ministers and laity.

In his book *They Said Yes: A Life in Missions, Robert K. & Evangeline Rodenbush,* William Turner recounts the inception of the Associate in Missions (AIM) program.

> The genesis of the AIM program further emerged from the flight lounge at the airport in Salt Lake City where Robert and Evangeline waited between flights. They could not help but notice dozens of young Mormon missionaries returning from two-year overseas "missions" as they were being met by their waiting families. Why was the United Pentecostal Church International not enlisting its young people in short-term missions service? "I couldn't get the thought out of my mind," Robert said. Upon his return to St. Louis, he outlined the basic idea of what would become the Associates in Missions (AIM) program.

> Though the idea had obvious merits, there were concerns by some members of Global Missions administrative committee and also by the board. The concern was that the short-term missions program would draw off funds from the expanding PIM program. It was decided to do a pilot program and accept the appointment of a couple of volunteers in this experimental program.
>
> One of the first two volunteers was Linda Revell (Poitras), from Alabama to Nigeria. Both young women proved to be productive and outstanding volunteers, and both proved the point that local church financial support of short-term missionaries did not adversely affect overall financial support for career missionaries. Linda Revell later met her future husband, James Poitras, when they were both serving on AIM to Nigeria. After their marriage they were appointed as career missionaries to Nigeria, and later to Ghana.
>
> Robert observed that, more often than not, young people who receive on-the-field training as an AIM volunteer serving under the leadership of veteran missionaries prove to be more adaptable to a team-concept of missions work. He further observed that, occasionally, missionaries who never served on AIM and were appointed later in their missionary careers were less adaptable to a team format of leadership. (pp. 142–43)

Today, almost all candidates meeting the Global Missions Board have served on AIM and the associate missionary program. In 2018 the General Conference approved a name change from AIM to short-term missions (STM). This was due to so many new programs being developed. The online landing page for all short-term missions programs through Global Missions is gmstm.net.

Associate Missionary Program

The Associate Missionary Program (AMP) is an AIM upgrade which allows for a larger budget and a potential of two to three months of deputation every two years. Requirements are a year on the field as an AIMer and ministerial license with the UPCI. Many AMPers continue on to become fully appointed missionaries.

Internship

Started in the summer of 2017, the STM intern program has made it possible to continue the expansion of STM programs. Interns assist with application processing, filing of paperwork, posting of reports to our websites, and other projects as needed.

Are you looking for long-term involvement with global missions? Start with a short-term missions endeavor, follow the Lord's leading to the next right step, and keep moving on from there. Searching for the will of God for your life? Look no more. The will of God is as simple as discovering and doing the next right step. Our history intercepts and intertwines with your future! We are probing and building a community of laborers while providing a pathway to the ripened harvest. Meet you in the field!

Notes

Introduction

1. Daniel Scott, *The Evolving World of Foreign Missions* (Hazelwood, MO: Foreign Missions Division, United Pentecostal Church International, 2009), 19.
2. Scott, 36.
3. Mary Wallace, compiler, *Profiles of Pentecostal Missionaries* (Hazelwood, MO: Word Aflame Press, 1986).
4. Scott, 67.

Chapter 1—Else Lund Story

1. Scott, 136.

Chapter 2—China, Before and After 1945

1. Kathryn E. Hendricks, "China Today," *Pentecostal Herald* (December 1949): 9.
2. Wallace, 323.
3. Wallace, 325.
4. Wallace, 328.
5. Wallace, 328.
6. Wallace, 330.
7. Wallace, 331.
8. Wallace, 332.
9. Wallace, 332.
10. Wallace, 341.
11. Wallace, 337.
12. Wallace, 338–39.
13. Wallace, 340.
14. Wallace, 340.
15. Scott, 67.
16. Scott, 67.
17. Wallace, 342.
18. Wallace, 343.
19. Wallace, 348.

20. Prior to 2011, UPCI Global Missions was known as the Foreign Missions Division, and many of the historical references in the book retain that designation.
21. Scott, 164.
22. Scott, 20.
23. Scott, 303.
24. Wallace, 303–04.
25. Wallace, 307.
26. Scott, 37.
27. Scott, 246.

Chapter 3—India

1. Scott, 24
2. Scott, 19.
3. William D. Turner, *India to the World: The Missionary Pilgrimage of Harry E. Scism* (Indianapolis, IN: Voice & Vision Publications, 2017), 81.
4. Scott, 19.
5. Turner, 81.
6. Scott, 24.
7. Turner, 83.
8. Stanley W. Chambers, "Dorothy McCarty at Home with the Lord," *Pentecostal Herald* (September 1947): 9.
9. Telie Dover, UPCI Order of the Faith, accessed 15 December 2023, https://oof.upci.org.
10. Turner, *India to the World* (Voice & Visions Publications, 2017), 158–59.
11. Turner, *India to the World*, 160–61.
12. Telie Dover Greer, *Telie: My Story* (Ruston, LA: Dover & Greer, 1993), 113.
13. Turner, *India to the World*, 162–63.
14. Turner, *India to the Worl*d, 164–65.
15. Order of the Faith 2019, Telie Dover Greer, Biographical Sketch (Weldon Spring, MO: United Pentecostal Church International, 2019).
16. Scott, 420.
17. Access to Global Mission files, Janice Leaman (April 12, 2023).
18. Scott, 217.
19. William D. Turner, *India to the World*, vi.

Chapter 4—East Asia (Japan and South Korea)

1. Wallace, 87.
2. Wallace, 87.
3. Wallace, 90.
4. Wallace, 91.
5. Wallace, 99.
6. Frances L. Munsey, "Only One Life," Unpublished manuscript (n.d.).

Chapter 5—South Asia (Bangladesh and Pakistan)

1. William D. Turner, Miracle: *The Missionary Life of Don and Saundra Hanscom* (Crawfordsville, IN: Peaceful Valley Publications, 2021), 73.
2. Turner, *The Missionary Life of Don and Saundra Hanscom*, 74.
3. Turner, *The Missionary Life of Don and Saundra Hanscom*, 73–4.
4. Frances Foster and Lynda Allison, *Around the World with Jesus: The Frances Foster Story* (Portland, OR: Apostolic Book Publishers, 1992), 146, 164.
5. Foster, 74–5.
6. Lois Corcoran, *He Leadeth Me: Autobiography of a Missionary to Pakistan* (Hazelwood, MO: Word Aflame Press, 1991), 100.
7. Corcoran, 105–6.
8. Corcoran, 105–6.
9. Corcoran, 105–6.
10. Corcoran, 108.
11. Corcoran, 109–10.
12. Corcoran, 116–18.
13. Frances Foster, 174–75.
14. Foster, 181.
15. Foster, 163.
16. Foster, 191–95.
17. Foster, 191–95.
18. Foster, 255–64.

Chapter 6—Southeast Asia (Thailand, Java, and Tonga)

1. Scott, 41.
2. Read a detailed account of Billy and Shirley Cole's Thailand missionary work in *SENT! Volume 1.*
3. Elly Hansen and Mary Wallace, *Following Jesus All the Way: Elly* (Hazelwood, MO: Word Aflame Press, 1987), 33.
4. Hansen and Wallace, 34–35.
5. Hansen and Wallace, 36.
6. Hansen and Wallace, 36.
7. Hansen and Wallace, 37.
8. Hansen and Wallace, 37–50.
9. Hansen and Wallace, 45–46.
10. Hansen and Wallace, 46.
11. Hansen and Wallace, 47, 95.
12. Hansen and Wallace, 50–51.
13. Hansen and Wallace, 51–53.
14. Hansen and Wallace, 53.
15. Hansen and Wallace, 56.
16. Hansen and Wallace, 58–59.
17. Hansen and Wallace, 59.
18. Hansen and Wallace, 64–65.
19. Hansen and Wallace, 67.
20. Hansen and Wallace, 67.
21. Burk, *Apostolic Pioneers in Mission*s (United Pentecostal Church International, 2012), 60.
22. Hansen and Wallace, 104.
23. Hansen and Wallace, 105.
24. Hansen and Wallace, 107.
25. Hansen and Wallace, 107.
26. Hansen and Wallace, 107.
27. Hansen and Wallace, 107.
28. Hansen and Wallace, 109.
29. Hansen and Wallace, 119.
30. Dorsey Burk, *Apostolic Pioneers in Missions* (United Pentecostal Church International, 2012), 61.
31. Burk, *Apostolic Pioneers in Missions*, 62.
32. Burk, *Apostolic Pioneers in Missions*, 62.

33. Scott, 78.
34. Scott, 84.
35. Scott, 92.
36. Crystal Reece, email correspondence with Darline Royer (17 May 2023).
37. Crystal Reece, *Island Splashes* (Bloomington, IN: Westbow Press, 2013).

Chapter 7—Liberia

1. Burk, *Apostolic Pioneers in Missions*, 69.
2. Scott, 104.
3. Wallace, *Profiles of Pentecostal Missionaries*, 146.
4. Wallace, 175.
5. Scott, 93.
6. Pauline Gruse with Charles Clanton, *I Surrender All* (Hazelwood, MO: Word Aflame Press, 1979), 141.
7. Burk, *Apostolic Pioneers in Missions*, 52.
8. Gruse, 28.
9. Gruse, 102.
10. Gruse, 104.
11. Gruse, chapter 7.
12. Gruse, 122, 126.
13. Gruse, 127.
14. Gruse, 139.
15. Gruse, 142.
16. Gruse, 146.
17. Gruse, chapter 11.
18. Gruse, 164.
19. Gruse, 166.
20. Gruse, 175–76.
21. Gruse, 178.
22. Gruse, 190.
23. Gruse, 225–26.
24. Gruse, 230–31.
25. Gruse, 234–35.
26. Sam Latta, *Liberia Sweet* (n.d.), 27, 14.
27. Gruse, 294–95.
28. Scott, 135.
29. Gruse, 306–07.

30. Scott, 251.
31. Burk, *Apostolic Pioneers in Missions*, 54.
32. Gruse, 289.
33. Scott, 91.
34. Wallace, 245.
35. Scott, 193.
36. Scott, 223.
37. Scott, 95.
38. Scott, 95.
39. Scott, 168.

Chapter 8—East Africa (Kenya, Tanzania, Malawi)

1. Bobbye Wendell, phone conversation with Darline Royer (2023).
2. Darline Royer, *SENT! Volume 3, A History of UPCI Global Missions, Africa* (Weldon Spring, MO: Word Aflame Press, 2022), 247, 281–292.
3. Summary about Loice Sparks by Carolyn Simoneaux, veteran missionary to Tanzania.

Chapter 9—Central and Southern Africa (Gabon, South Africa, Lesotho)

1. Colleen Carter's story is a compilation of content from the Global Missions website, conversations with Colleen, written material provided by her, and information from her social media posts.
2. Karen Poole, email correspondence (26 October 2023).
3. Karen wrote her story in first person and then collaborated with Darline Royer in compiling this condensed account of her transition to single missionary life.
4. Scott, 79.
5. Carrie Lee Powledge Eastridge obituary, accessed 9 December 2023, www.findagrave.com.
6. "Remembering Nona Freeman," Facebook post (accessed 17 April 2023).
7. Carrie Lee Powledge Eastridge obituary.
8. Scott, 256.

9. "Remembering Nona Freeman."
10. Scott, 99.
11. Scott, 256.
12. Scott, 119.
13. Carrie Lee Powledge Eastridge obituary.

Chapter 10— Zimbabwe, Bophuthatswana

1. *1984 Foreign Missions Story* (Foreign Missions Division UPCI), 26.
2. Burk, *Apostolic Pioneers in Missions*, 117.
3. Lesley Kelley, email correspondence (28 March 2023 and 8 April 2023).
4. Lesley Kelley, email correspondence.

Chapter 11—Alaska

1. Grace Yadon Wiens, *Unto You and Your Children* (Hazelwood, MO: Word Aflame Press, 1977; Fourth printing in Chiang Mai, Thailand, 2004).
2. Scott, 71.
3. Scott, 78.
4. Janice Leaman, text message (5 September 2023).
5. Scott, 80.
6. Grace Yadon Wiens, *One Room Cabin* (Booklet, n.d.).
7. Scott, 93.

Chapter 12 —El Salvador, Honduras, Belize

1. *Foreign Missions Insight* 1997, 50.

Chapter 13—Guatemala

1. Special thanks to Melinda Poitras for writing Lynne's story for this book.
2. UPCIGlobalMissions.org (accessed September 2023).
3. Lynne Jewett and Melinda Poitras, *Disasters Minister: True Stories of Living in Faith through All of Life's Disasters*, Kindle Edition (Amazon.com Services LLC, 2020).

Chapter 14—Brazil

1. Scott, 171.
2. Bennie DeMerchant and Dolly McElhaney, *Full Throttle! The Missionary Story of Bennie and Theresa DeMerchant* (Hazelwood, MO: Word Aflame Press, 2008), 169–79.
3. Scott, 228.
4. Scott, 228.
5. Scott, 255.

Chapter 15—Ecuador

1. Lucile Farmer and Mary Loudermilk, *A Willing Heart* (Hood River, OR: Alpha Bible Publications, 1991).
2. Farmer, 149.
3. Farmer, 153.
4. Farmer, 156.
5. Farmer, 157.
6. Farmer, 177.
7. Farmer, 187.
8. Farmer, 188–89.
9. Farmer, 189.
10. Farmer, 190.
11. Farmer, 191.
12. Farmer, 193.
13. Farmer, 195.
14. Farmer, 196–97.
15. Farmer, 198–99.
16. Farmer, 199.
17. Farmer, 205.
18. Farmer, 204.
19. Farmer, 203.
20. Farmer, 204.
21. Farmer, 210–11.
22. Farmer, 224.
23. Farmer, 233–34.
24. Farmer, 239–40.
25. Farmer, 240.

Chapter 16—Colombia

1. Scott, 78.
2. Scott, 66.
3. Scott, 78.
4. Scott, 207.
5. *1984 Foreign Missions Story* (Foreign Missions Division UPCI), 64.
6. Dorsey L. Burk, *Foreign Missions Story–1986* (Foreign Missions Division UPCI), 85.
7. Scott, 80.
8. Scott, 361.
9. Scott, 100.
10. Scott, 101.
11. Scott, 361.
12. Scott, 223–24.
13. Scott, 361.
14. Scott, 411.

Chapter 17—Portugal, France, Morocco, Algeria, Tunisia

1. Rachel Hattabaugh, email correspondence with Darline Royer (5 May 2023).
2. Trecina Anderson, Zoom Interview, Divine Connection, 15 Feb 2022, https://youtube/ HVMTvoETZ70.
3. Trecina Anderson, email correspondence with Elizabeth Turner (10 March 2022).
4. Trecina Anderson, Zoom interview.
5. Trecina Anderson Zoom interview (15 February 2022).
6. *Foreign Missions Insights-1999* (UPCI Foreign Missions Division), 99.
7. *Insight*, Foreign Missions Directory, 3rd Edition, 132.
8. *Insight*, Foreign Missions Directory, 3rd Edition, 132.

Chapter 18—Switzerland and Russia, Jordan

1. Personal account by Amber Hackenbruch.
2. William Turner, *The Church on Godless Lane: Missionary Stories from Russia and the Former Soviet Union* (Peaceful Valley Publication, 2009), 86.
3. Turner, *The Church on Godless Lane*, 87.
4. Turner, *The Church on Godless Lan*e, 87–88.
5. Turner, *The Church on Godless Lane*, 90.
6. Turner, *The Church on Godless Lane*, 93.

Chapter 19—Jordan and an Access Challenged Nation

1. Jason Crumpacker, phone conversation (October 2023).
2. Michelle Hancock, phone conversation with Darline Royer (10 October 2023).
3. Michelle Hancock, text message to Darline Royer (10 October 2023).
4. Bonnie L., email to Darline Royer (6 November 2023).
5. Bonnie provided the details for her story.

Bibliography

Burk, Dorsey L. *Apostolic Pioneers in Missions.* United Pentecostal Church International, 2012.

Burk, Dorsey, compiler and editor. *Insight*, 3rd Edition. Foreign Missions Division, United Pentecostal Church International, 2002

Corcoran, Lois. *He Leadeth Me: Autobiography of a Missionary to Pakistan.* Hazelwood, MO: Word Aflame Press, 1991.

DeMerchant, Bennie, and Dolly McElhaney. *Full Throttle! The Missionary Story of Bennie and Theresa DeMerchant*. Hazelwood, MO: Word Aflame Press, 2008.

Farmer, Lucile, and Mary Loudermilk. *A Willing Heart.* Hood River, OR: Alpha Bible Publications, 1991.

Foster, Frances, and Lynda Allison. *Around the World with Jesus: The Frances Foster Story.* Portland, OR: Apostolic Book Publishers, 1992.

Greer, Telie Dover. *Telie: My Story.* Ruston, LA: Dover & Greer Publishers, 1993.

Gruse, Pauline, with Charles Clanton. *I Surrender All: The Autobiography of a Courageous Missionary.* Hazelwood, MO: Word Aflame Press, 1979.

Hansen, Elly, and Mary Wallace. *Following Jesus All the Way: Elly*. Hazelwood, MO: Word Aflame Press, 1987.

Latta, Sam. *Liberia Sweet*, n.d.

Markham, Bonnie. *Sarah and Her Missionary Daughters: Personal Glimpses into the Lives of Thirty Missionary Ladies.* Hazelwood, MO: Word Aflame Press, 1998.

Order of the Faith 2019. Telie Dover Greer. Biographical Sketch. Weldon Springs, MO: United Pentecostal Church International, 2019.

Reece, Crystal G. *Island Splashes.* Bloomington, IN: WestBow Press, 2013.

Scott, Daniel. *The Evolving World of Foreign Missions.* Hazelwood, MO: Foreign Missions Division, United Pentecostal Church International, 2009.

Turner, William D. *India to the World: The Missionary Pilgrimage of Harry E. Scism.* Voice & Vision Publications, 2017.

Turner, William D. *Miracle: The Missionary Life of Don and Saundra Hanscom.* Crawfordsville, IN: Peaceful Valley Publications, 2021.

Turner, William D. *The Church on Godless Lane: Missionary Stories from Russia and the Former Soviet Union.* Peaceful Valley Publications, 2009.

Wallace, Mary, compiler. *Profiles of Pentecostal Missionaries.* St. Louis: Word Aflame Press, 1986.

Yadon Wiens, Grace, *Unto You and Your Children.* Hazelwood, MO: Word Aflame Press, 1977; Fourth printing—Chiang Mai, Thailand, 2004.

Yadon Wiens, Grace. *One Room Cabin.* Unpublished manuscript, n.d.